I Remember When Mom . . .

I Remember When Mom . . .

Memories and Stories about *Mothers*

Collected by Louise Betts Egan

Ariel Books

Andrews McMeel Publishing

Kansas City

03 04 05 06 07 FFG 10 9 8 7 6 5 4 3 2 1

Library of Congress Cataloging-in-Publication Data

I remember when mom . . . : memories and stories about mothers /
collected by Louise Betts Egan.
   p. cm.
ISBN 0-7407-3312-5
1.Mothers. 2. Mother and child. I. Betts, Louise.

HQ759.I64   2003
306.87–dc21

2002035621

*To all mothers,
mothers-in-law, stepmothers, and
"other mothers," past, present, and future.*

— L B E

Forward

Throughout time, mothers have been called upon to be the family historians, to remember the cute, funny, or momentous things their children did. Rarely are children called upon to remember the same about their mothers—and yet the stories are there, abundantly there, waiting to be told. This book captures some of those stories. On each page is a picture, in words, of a mother. Here, sons and daughters of all ages and from all over the United States and the world tell something about their mothers—the funny things they did, the advice they gave, and the sacrifices they made, as well as the comfort and joy they provided. For many contributors, the stories tapped memories long put away, or put into words the thank-yous that had gone unmentioned. The one thing each story has in common, of course, is the love—however simple or complex—for this most unique of beings, Mom.

I lived in Greenwich Village when I was very young, and I can remember walking to preschool with my mom, who would carry me while we sang songs. They weren't your regular songs, because Mom likes to speak different languages. So we sang "Imsa Vimsa Spindal" (that's "Itsy Bitsy Spider") in Swedish, and "Alouette" in French, and "La Cucaracha" in Spanish. Then she would make up one in English about me, and I would sing the next verse about her.

After school was over, we would go to the bakery next door to my preschool and get a blueberry muffin. I learned to skip that year and we would skip together until Mom got tired and I ran the rest of the way home.

Nick, 10, Saint Louis, Missouri

I grew up in Guatemala, and whenever it rained, it was also cold. So when I came back from school at the end of a rainy day, my mother would be waiting there for me with a cup of hot chocolate. I appreciated that, though I pretty much took it for granted.

That is, until I moved away from home. After being away five years, I went back to visit, and it was cold and rainy when I landed. I got off the plane and there was Mom, waiting for me with a huge smile—and a cup of hot chocolate.

Now I live in New York, and whenever it rains, I think of that special combination of sweetness and warmth.

Maria, 25, New Rochelle, New York

$\mathscr{M}$y mom says friends still tell her how much fun they had at my dad's fortieth birthday party—which was more than thirty years ago in Brooklyn, New York. Back then, though she worked full-time, Mom was still able to come up with a theme and clever invitation, which she honed on the phone with her friends. I remember them laughing and spitting out ideas, some good and some hilarious.

The theme was "Come as a Kid." The invitation was written on torn notebook paper. Dads came in shorts with suspenders, wore beanies, and carried big lollipops; moms came in frilly baby-doll dresses and wore their hair in exaggerated ponytails and bows. My brother and I, ages twelve and nine, wore our parents' adult clothes.

There was a pretty-baby contest, pin the tail on the donkey, and other kid games. People just laughed all night, and went home with goody bags.

Barbara, 39, Rome, Italy

$\mathcal{M}$om is a lawyer and the one who works in our family. Dad never could seem to hold down a job for long, and I think he eventually gave up. When Mom and Dad divorced, Dad used Mom's job against her, saying she was never home enough to take care of us, whereas he was at home all the time. Well, yes, Dad was home—smoking dope and sitting at the computer. My sisters and I were really worried that Dad would get custody, because the judge thought Dad's argument was good (and maybe the judge didn't like women lawyers). Fortunately, Mom went to court for us and won.

Linda, 19, Charleston, South Carolina

$\mathcal{M}$ost parents do not want their children to be out late dancing. My mother is different: She forced me to go to school dances. It was not that she wanted me out of the house or that she wanted me to be interested in boys. It was simply that she wanted me to be sociable, something that did not come naturally to me.

Mom knew that I disliked school and that I hated dances, but she had something for every argument I possessed. I'd say, "I've already been to the dances and I know that I don't like them." She'd say, "Maybe you'll like it this time."

Somehow I would always end up at the dance. Once, I was standing around with my friends, when I started complaining about how Mom had forced me to come. Much to my surprise, all of my friends' moms had forced them to come to the dance as well. It was at this point that I realized my mom wasn't so weird after all.

Jacqueline, 14, Larchmont, New York

$\mathcal{M}$om went to a one-room schoolhouse in Enid, Oklahoma, from first through seventh grades, before going to more established schools for higher education. But her favorite years, the ones she talked about most when I was young, were the early ones spent at what she called "country school."

Spring Valley School, set between wheat fields and the highway, was a mile walk from her home. The school was a simple white frame building with a small belfry and a barn for students who rode horses to school. Inside were chairs with attached writing boards, a desk for the one teacher, and a chalkboard on the wall. The student body, never more than twenty children, spanned kindergarten through eighth grade and included Mom's brothers, cousins, and neighboring farm children. A water pump outside, a woodstove inside, the three Rs, and two recesses every day. They were simple, nurturing years.

Louise, 45, Emmaus, Pennsylvania

$\mathcal{M}$y mother, a beautiful dresser, was always proud that she had the first charge account at Neiman Marcus's flagship store in Dallas when she was a young woman in Arkansas. She never left the house without looking well-groomed. When she lived in Chicago, she always wore her hat and gloves, and would be mortified at the way people dress today.

Virginia, 65, Shaker Heights, Ohio

$\mathcal{M}$y mother was very beautiful and, in terms of having close, open discussions about intimate matters with her daughter, ahead of her time. This was 1939, in Vienna, as war descended on Europe. I was sixteen and would soon be immigrating to America without my parents. I would also be leaving my boyfriend, with whom I was madly in love. The two of us wanted to consummate our relationship and I asked Mother what I should do.

"Wait," she replied. "When you see each other again, you'll be older and will know what it means." I took her advice.

After the war, my boyfriend found me. By then, I was a college graduate, just starting out in New York City. He had been in Argentina, on an *estancia* [farm], and wanted me to go back with him. I said no—I just couldn't change lives again—and we parted forever.

I think my mother's advice to wait ultimately gave me the power to let go, hard as it was.

Gerda, 80, Providence, Rhode Island

$\mathcal{T}$he smell of peroxide and hair dye, like hot paint mixed with strawberry jam, regularly filled the rooms of my childhood. When my mother said, "I need to give myself a touch-up today," and headed for the kitchen, I took my place across from her, hands folded on our white Formica table, and watched her draw out those small glass bottles of Clairol, familiar as containers of homogenized milk, from the depths of her huge gray case.

When everything was laid out on the table, Mom unfurled her black plastic cape and, like Clark Kent becoming Superman, became Gloria the Hairdresser. *Zzzzzip* went the black plastic tail comb, and a part straight as death ripped across her scalp above the ear. Thick burgundy hair dye, spread with a flat-bristled brush, made a lapping, suction sound. Slurp, slurp, spread, spread. *Zzzzzip* with the tail comb, slicing another deadeye part precisely half an inch above the first one, as the thrilling smell of touch-up began to fill our tiny apartment.

Jackie, 44, New York, New York

$\mathscr{I}$ was twenty-four years old, had held two jobs since college, had moved 3,000 miles away from home—and I was homesick, depressed, and wondering what I was doing with my life.

"I want to come home," I told my mother over the phone.

Mom flew out to help me with packing and then served as my steady companion for four days as I drove the two of us cross-country, away from sunny California, through tiny Midwestern towns, past kitschy souvenir stands, cornfields, factories, and cities—until we reached New York and home. We drove during the day and stayed in modest motels at night; I enjoyed the simple structure of only having to drive from point A to point B each day, and Mom was the friendly, solid company that I needed.

Ultimately, Mom was that perfect bridge between the end of my biggest life stumble and the start of a fresh, new chapter that has been going on track ever since.

Lisa, 46, East Greenwich, Rhode Island

$\mathcal{S}$mile," Mom says as she hops in the backseat for a quick "before" snapshot. I imagine we are five and seven, getting comfortable in the way back of the tan Pontiac station wagon for a long trip.

We could be headed off for a day at the beach, or maybe farther, to Maine, Cape Cod, or Washington, D.C., but our luggage is not packed to the roof and we do not have our pillows for napping. More likely, we are heading out for one of Mom's day trips to a local attraction—the game farm or the aquarium or a museum.

I imagine the cooler packed with Mom-made bologna-and-cheese sandwiches on Wonder bread; Lay's potato chips; packages of Devil Dogs; juicy black plums; and Cokes—our "menu" for such special occasions. We look so happy in the way back, as we almost always were in the car, eager to greet the adventure that lay ahead, ready to hold Mom's hands when we arrived.

Keri, 31, Bethlehem, Connecticut

$\mathcal{M}$om said her eighth-grade teacher used to call her a "ditzy blonde." Mom loves to laugh and have a good time, but ditzy (and, by now, blonde) she's not. Mom is a go-getter, but one with an enormous heart, who goes to bat for things she believes in.

For years, Mom was a newspaper reporter, working at the metro desk and then editing national news. Her boss liked her style of asking tough questions in a nice way, one that often broke stories. Now Mom has her own successful media consulting business, with clients nationwide asking for her advice.

Even so, Mom found time to head my Girl Scout troop, become a deacon at church, and help raise funds for local issues. Before I was born, when Vietnamese refugees moved into our area, Mom signed up to help a family, and we're still in touch with them. At a crowded community board meeting, Mom can stand at the back of the room, raise her hand, and ask a good question.

Mom's always there for us and others, always amazing.

Adrienne, 17, Hagerstown, Maryland

$\mathcal{I}$ was an awkward, shy sixteen-year-old who, like other girls, dreaded the day that a certain crowd of mean boys would pick on me. That day came and I cried my eyes out when I got home from school. My mom hugged me, wiped my tears away, told me I was beautiful and that what they said could never be true.

I was still skeptical.

Then Mom told me I should say a prayer for them.

Waste a prayer on those jerks?!

Mom said that there must be something really sad in their lives for them to want to make other people feel bad, too, so they needed my prayers.

Reluctantly, I promised Mom that I would try. To this day, I think of those boys and say a prayer for them. I'm not sure if any of their pains were healed, but I'm certain that this has helped me and that I am a better person because I prayed for them.

Maureen, 42, East Islip, New York

Little Women is one of my favorite books. As a girl, I first read my mother's treasured copy from her childhood, with its musty smell and brittle pages. Even as a teenager, I used the girls in the book as a type of shorthand in describing to my mother what a certain classmate was like. For example, if I said, "She's a Jo," or, "She's such an Amy!" Mom would know exactly what I meant.

The day I moved into my first apartment, Mom brought me a housewarming gift: a lovely, new, hardbound edition of our favorite book by Louisa May Alcott. Mom figured I'd need one to take me through the years to come.

Shelby, 26, Falls Church, Virginia

I was one of three sisters growing up in the seventies, with a single mom. No, we didn't have "hair of gold," but I did long for Mom to meet a man like Mike Brady on TV, so we could be like the Brady Bunch.

Mom dated occasionally, but she never met her Mike. Instead, she poured her efforts into her work (executive secretary) and her three daughters. I saw how hard she worked at giving us clothes and birthday parties and getting each of us through college. My sisters and I helped out by baby-sitting and getting good grades, but I wish we could have done more, so Mom could have had more simple moments and more fun. She always felt bad that she could not give us a real father, and I think it ate her up inside. What she did give me was love, compassion, and a foundation to start my own life. I wish she were here to realize that—and to appreciate her first grandchild.

Heather, 33, Lexington, Kentucky

$\mathcal{M}$y mom has always been fascinated by different cultures. As kids, we were lucky enough to visit various exotic places all over the world. On one vacation in Tangiers, Morocco, we were continually warned that it was not safe to venture into the "medina," or the labyrinth of streets that led to the marketplace. Taking no heed, my mother marched into the narrow alleyways, sketchbook under her arm, introducing us at a tender age to the delights of haggling and bartering for souvenirs.

Soon Mom had struck up a friendship with a young student, who invited our family to his sister's wedding the next day. I will never forget the amazing sight of the bride, daubed in henna and dressed in her ceremonial robes, riding a camel!

What my mother passed on to me is how rewarding taking a risk can be, when you show an interest in people and places, and also, that "different" can be interesting and not necessarily strange.

Josh, 28, Halifax, Nova Scotia, Canada

$\mathcal{P}$ardon me while I gush about my mother-in-law—who is a friend, confidante, and loving mother, and, who as a grandmother, cannot do enough for or think more about our children.

She lives far away, but, like Santa Claus, she knows when we're sleeping and what we're doing when we're awake. She keeps in touch by phone and through the mail. Thoughtfully chosen birthday cards and presents arrive days beforehand.

We visit my mother-in-law once a year for six days. When we arrive, she has filled the cupboard and fridge with our favorite foods and necessities. She plans outings and does them with us enthusiastically. At the grocery store, she's always hoping to run into a friend to show off her grandchildren. Throughout the day, we laugh, talk, make meals; even playing bingo is fun with her. Then she'll stay up late at night to talk with her son or watch the show he's watching.

Stand-up comedians love to pick on mothers-in-law. With mine, they'd have no material. She's a saint!

Nicolette, 38, Kansas City, Kansas

$\mathcal{M}$um was on her deathbed—and this story shows it's never too late to let loose. Mum was a minister's daughter, and the one thing she hated in life was bad language. Actually, Mum put up with my father for forty years, which was a lot worse than bad language—something my mother finally acknowledged to me in the hospital.

While I was there visiting and hearing her confess all these things to me, a nurse walked in and discreetly left a bedpan for Mum to use, then walked out. A while later, Mum needed to use the bedpan and it was so awkward and awful, and all of the sudden Mum grumbled, "Oh, I hate these *!##* things!" I shrieked when I heard that word come out of her mouth. The nurses came rushing in, but Mum and I were laughing too hard to explain.

Kate, 36, Santa Fe, New Mexico

$\mathcal{M}$om was brought up Protestant, and Dad, Jewish, so when they had my brother, Rick, and me, we celebrated Christmas, Hanukkah, Easter, and Passover. Even so, we didn't go to church or synagogue—Mom and Dad were not that religious.

That ended when, in a car pool discussion, Mom heard Rick (then age seven) say, regarding what religion we were, "We're not really anything." Shortly after that, Mom had Dad taking us to temple on Saturdays and Sunday school the next day. My Jewish grandparents lived nearby and sometimes they took us. You could say that this made Dad "rediscover his roots."

Meanwhile, Mom began overcompensating for her holidays: more decorations, more cookies, more presents and holiday clothes, until it got too crazy for her. Mom converted to Judaism ten years ago and it has made all the difference. Now holidays have more meaning, with all of us celebrating one religion's traditions, and I like going to temple as a family. I'm grateful to her for making that choice.

Zev, 17, Alexandria, Virginia

$\mathcal{M}$om has always been creative but not very precise, and she definitely does not listen to other people. She had just bought a camera to take pictures at a cousin's wedding. We're from Iran, and the Persian ceremony was very elaborate. Mom admired the setup enormously. She wanted to take all sorts of photos, close-ups, angles, etc., to get ideas for a wedding she was going to arrange some months later.

So Mom got busy clicking away, squatting, doing verticals, pressing herself between walls and furniture, when I noticed something and called out to her.

"Mom!"

"Just a minute."

"Mom, it's important!" I tried once more.

"Can't you see I'm busy?"

"This is important."

"Okay, what do you want?"

"Just to say your lens cap is on."

Massoumeh, 42, Geneva, Switzerland

One of Mom's favorite stories is the one about my senior prom. I was class president but something of a free spirit, too. I rode a unicycle to sports events, made funny announcements over the loudspeaker, and was generally known as a jokester, the kind that makes teachers roll their eyes.

On prom night, Mom was one of the chaperones. She was standing near the doorway to the gym before it began, when she heard the vice principal say to a teacher, "Here comes that screwball, Egan. Sheesh—what a nut case!" (I was wearing a top hat and tails, and my date had on a large pink boa.) Mom looked over to the two, wondering if they knew she was Mrs. Egan. Guessing that they did not, she looked down at her toes and laughed and laughed.

Rob, 39, Framingham, Massachusetts

When I think of Mom, I think of seeing her face in the kitchen window as I came up the drive, riding my bike home from school. Day after day, year after year, Mom would be in the kitchen making dinner when I came home.

Dinners were important in our family. We were five children, plus Mom and Dad, and every evening we would eat together—a meat dish, vegetable, and salad (dessert was usually up for grabs).

During vacations, I noticed that sometimes Mom would start browning meat right after breakfast. Other times, she'd ask with a touch of desperation, "What should we have for dinner?" Back then, there was no fast-food option or pizza delivery service. Dinner was made from scratch every night.

Now that I'm a mom and making dinners myself, I can appreciate just *how many* dinners she made—and why, once Dad died, packaged frozen dinners became her daily luxury.

Jamie, 46, Nashville, Tennessee

$\mathcal{M}$y parents, both immigrants from the Ukraine, worked hard at the luncheonette they owned. Nearly every August, they took a few weeks off to go to a resort in the mountains. One of Mom's favorite stories was when I was three years old and Dad had to stay behind, and the two of us went on to the resort.

One night, we went to the dance and were sitting on a bench in the back, when a man approached my mother and asked her to dance. To reassure me that she was not going far, Mom said she would dance with him right there, where we were sitting. She got up and walked a few steps toward him.

I thought, "Nope," leaped off the bench, and grabbed the back of Mom's dress. She turned around, and I said, "You got a husband!"

Mom thanked the man politely and the two of us sat back down. Even though Mom loved to dance, that night it was not to be. In Dad's absence, my immediate reflex was to protect our exclusive family domain.

Henry, 64, New York, New York

$\mathcal{M}$y mom is an all-or-nothing sort of person. When I needed her help and she was there to give it to me, it was great. I loved it when Mom helped me with schoolwork, or gave me advice, or had nice, long mother-daughter talks, or even went shopping with me. But when Mom was giving her all at work, I might not see her for days or might not really talk with her for longer than that. It's easier now that I'm in college, because I'm not at home to miss her. We'll make a date to talk and we both try our best not to break it.

Elise, 19, Augusta, Maine

$\mathcal{W}$hen I was a girl, my friends would tell me, "Your mom is so cute!" The other moms would tell me she was "charming." I knew what they meant. Mom was from Italy—and so different, with her thick accent and European customs.

It took me a while to realize just how proud of her I was, having to deal with values and ways so unlike those of her native land. She always tried so hard to fit in, bringing us to parties, attending school functions, and even volunteering with the PTA. My dad was always working and couldn't do these things with her.

Mom passed away a long time ago, but I haven't forgotten her sense of humor and her wonderful gift for storytelling. I still think of how she would react in a certain situation or how she might comfort me in stressful times. And I hope I can pass on to my own children some of her best qualities.

Tilde, 44, San Terenzo, Italy

I always loved my mother, but the first inkling I had that she was smart, too, occurred when I was about six years old. My older sister and I had had a fight and I was still burning mad. To get back at her, I bit myself on the arm, then ran off to my mother.

"Look what Claire did," I wailed, showing her the tooth marks on my arm. Oh, now Claire was going to get it! I thought.

Instead, my mom said, "Claire didn't do that. You did it to yourself. Look—those tooth marks on your arm are missing two front teeth—just like you! And Claire has her front teeth. Now, go to your room."

Helen, 19, Enid, Oklahoma

$\mathcal{I}$ was diagnosed with breast cancer at age thirty and Mom flew right out to be with me so my husband could continue going to work and to help take care of our baby. It's hard to describe how much Mom's care meant to me. It meant . . . everything.

Together, we read about different treatments and with my husband, too, figured out a course for me. We went for radiation and, as predicted, my hair fell out. I had always had thick, wavy black hair—a source of pride and a trait I got from my mother, who, by then, wore her hair short, but it still looked great.

One morning, I was tying a scarf around my head when Mom walked into my bedroom. She had a scarf tied around her head, and I made some comment about us being mistaken for twins. At which point, she removed her scarf to show her head, newly shorn to a stubble's length. I gasped. She smiled and said, "There's strength in unity."

Stephanie, 46, San Diego, California

*I*f you'd asked me last year to talk about my mom, I might have told you how she supported me in gymnastics and helped me get through the SATs. Or maybe I would have remembered the time on a camping trip when Mom fixed our collapsed tent in the pouring rain, only to have it collapse again—and how we laughed (and froze). But in many ways, I took life with Mom for granted.

Mom died six months ago, and I now feel flooded with all the things I could say about her. I miss her all-out, floor-shaking laugh. I miss her taking me out to Starbucks—just us girls. I miss hearing the sewing machine whirring late at night—the only time she had to pursue her hobby. I even miss hearing her gossip on the telephone with her friends—she had a million of them, all types of people.

I've been accepted to college, but how can I move on without hugging her good-bye?

Ginger, 18, Montclair, New Jersey

The jeans and shorts that my children favor for family outings are a far cry from the clothes that my twin sister and I wore for such occasions. A gifted seamstress, my mother would run up the most gorgeous matching party dresses in just two days! They would be in rich red lace with creamy silk under-skirts, or yellow taffeta, with matching bolero jackets. I smile when I see the photographs of my sibling and me—two peas in a pod in identical flowery sundresses and floppy hats made to match!

Now a mother myself, I think to myself, "How did Mum ever do all that?"

Lorna, 42, Woking, England

$\mathcal{O}$ur favorite place as children was a friend's farm, where the main attraction, in any season, was a large spring-fed pond. The first barely warm spring day would find my sister, at least a few friends, and me at the pond, attempting to fish. Of course, one of us would always "accidentally" fall in and require the rest of us to jump in to the rescue. We would arrive home, one soggy group of kids.

What was memorable about my mom at those times was the way she would smile and laugh at our antics. The aftermath of these escapades meant, for her, freezing children to be warmed and multiple loads of wet, muddy laundry. Yet she never got angry or complained. We were "just being kids."

Her example serves me well when my own son and his friends troop in dripping and cold from a romp in the snow. As I load the dryer one more time, I think of Mom and remember her patience with us "just being kids."

Pam, 47, Pine Bush, New York

$\mathcal{M}$om and her garden, her lovely garden, full of flowers that I mostly do not know the names of, and Mom in her two-piece bathing suit working among them on a hot summer afternoon. She grew up in Arizona during World War II and, I imagine, had had her fill of the dry, dusty rust-colored plateaus and foothills. The colorful wealth of flowers able to be grown in Wisconsin, where I grew up, seemed as extraordinary to her as a Thanksgiving banquet.

Botanical gardens were always a destination worth checking out, whether local or on vacation. She'd say, to convince us, "I think you'll really enjoy this." What I liked best was how happy these gardens made Mom feel. We almost always stopped for ice cream afterward—a rare event otherwise.

Around February, Mom would start planning her summer garden on graph paper, then she would order the seeds. Then came spring planting and summer's endless weeding—but along with it, quiet, color, order, and a fragrant beauty.

Felice, 40, Memphis, Tennessee

$\mathcal{M}$y parents divorced when I was twelve. Mom, who had no college education, was left struggling to support herself and us three preteen children. During high school, preppy fashion, with its Izod shirts and Brooks Brothers cachet, was the big craze—though an expensive one. I knew not to even ask Mom for any of that. I knew we couldn't afford it. But how I longed to have just one Izod shirt!

One day, Mom walked in from work and gave me a present: two Izod shirts. I was stunned. How did she know? I burst into tears, knowing how hard she must have worked to get them. I just couldn't imagine how Mom knew what those shirts meant to me—and still do.

Judy, 37, Larchmont, New York

*W*hen I was about fifteen, and my sister two years younger, our mother was stricken with cancer. She got really sick and went into the hospital. Things did not look good, but she surprised us. Mom came back home, got better, and even went back to work, living a good five years longer, until the disease reappeared and claimed her two years later.

At one point, Mom told me about this weird experience she'd had in the hospital, looking down on herself on the operating table and thinking, "I'm not ready to go! My girls need me!" In fact, the doctors had told us that Mom had died on the operating table but had been revived.

I was always sad that Mom had died so young and had suffered so much toward the end. Still, I feel like I won some extra years with her and keep the memory of her close to my heart.

Fiona, 35, East Brunswick, New Jersey

$\mathcal{M}$any years ago, I drove my mother, recently widowed, from Florida to Boston, where she would spend the summer. A fan of blues music, I mapped out a route that would take us along Highway 61, where many of the famous blues artists had lived and died. My mother didn't know anything about this music, but she was willing to learn.

We explored small, dusty towns, searched for obscure grave markers, and talked to townspeople in the diners where we ate. The blues portion of the drive would end in Memphis, at Elvis Presley's Graceland; as we drove, Mom read aloud a particularly lurid biography of Elvis Presley—an unusual but oddly entertaining "read-aloud."

We stopped briefly in New York, where I was living, and I introduced her to my girlfriend, who later became my wife.

Mom has always been a wonderful mom, but that drive stands out as a special time and great shared experience.

George, 48, Rutland, Vermont

$\mathcal{M}$y mom likes nothing better than a cup of tea, not just to start off the morning, but also to have in the afternoon. And she isn't even English—she's American. She just loves a hot cup of tea in the afternoon, even in summer: She says it's relaxing.

Her favorite teatimes are with a friend or two, even if it's just with a mom coming over to pick up her child from a play date. With someone to share a large pot of tea, Mom and her friends will sit around the kitchen table and just talk and laugh and talk some more and laugh some more. Maybe my friends and I will do that when we're older, but probably with diet soda.

Jenny, 15, Newton, Massachusetts

$\mathcal{M}$y mother had a 1945 Chrysler that she held on to into her seventies, when she couldn't drive anymore. I don't know why she was so attached to that car, but it never gave out. It was an anachronism on wheels. In fact, it was so old by the time she sold it in the late sixties to a local tattooed garage mechanic, it already had kitsch value. A few changes and flame decals later, Mom's car went from being an old jalopy to an ironic, souped-up, antique hot rod driven on the same streets by the well-satisfied grease monkey.

Bob, 72, Columbus, Georgia

$\mathcal{I}$ was writing a paper on the women's movement and I asked Mom how it had influenced her. Her turning point, she said, came when we were on vacation in Maine with my aunt, uncle, and their three kids, all ten of us in a large cabin on a lake. Mom and Aunt Jo were always up early with the babies, so breakfast started about six A.M. and ended hours later when my teenage cousin got up. Dad and Uncle Steve would go out for breakfast, then golf.

Lunchtime came, babies first, then us older ones making ourselves sandwiches and leaving a huge mess. Mom and Aunt Jo helped each other, one in the kitchen, the other watching the little ones.

One time, Mom was finally coming down to the beach with me, when Dad and Uncle Steve came in and asked, "What's for lunch?" They didn't ask it in a mean way, but Mom dropped my hand and stared at them.

Then she said, "Surprise me!" and walked out the door.

Dionne, 28, Carson City, Nevada

$\mathcal{W}$hen my older sister wore her denim overalls to middle school one day, the vice principal sent her home with a note saying she couldn't return until she changed into proper pants or a skirt or dress. This was during the mid-1970s.

Mom marched over to the vice principal's office (the school was just around the corner from our house) and argued with him until he gave in. For the rest of that school year, my sister was the only girl permitted to wear overalls to school. Eventually, the rule was expanded to include all students, but my mother was the one who started it all.

Sue, 40, Tubac, Arizona

$\mathscr{I}$ went to college close to where I grew up. As such, when it came time to doing my laundry every two weeks, it seemed right to have my mom drive in to do it, because "I had so much important studying to do."

Every other Friday, she would come in and get my laundry, clean it overnight, and bring it to me Saturday—but always with a cake for me and the guys. Being a cool college kid, I probably never thanked her. But I'll do it now: Thanks, Ma.

Jason, 41, Lincoln, Nebraska

$\mathcal{I}$ never thought of my mother as a "single, working mother," which she would be called today. She was simply Mama to me, which is what I called her in Russian, the language we spoke at home. She and my dad were Russian immigrants. They met in Paris after World War II, then came to America and settled in Jamaica, New York, in the tough, working-class neighborhood where I grew up, both street-smart and nurtured by the extended Russian community.

Dad died when I was ten. I begged Mama not to marry anyone else, to let our lives be just the two of us, and she complied. With her core of steel, Mama kept me from falling in with the wrong crowd, pushed me academically, and disciplined me when I strayed, which I did often.

I have achieved much in my life—all thanks to Mama. But she died too soon, before I could begin to give back all that she gave me.

Ivan, 46, Sea Cliff, New York

I loved to see Mum laugh, and the time most guaranteed to see that was when she was with her sister (my aunt) at family get-togethers. Something would always set them off—first they'd giggle, then try to stop, knowing how it annoyed my uncle. But that just made it worse. The giggle became suppressed laughter and then—*boom!* They would shake with laughter, tears streaming down their faces, and they would set the whole room (except my uncle) to laughing uncontrollably. Either my mum or my aunt would have to leave the room before things could calm down.

This happened sometimes two or three times a day during a weekend visit. They felt bad about disrupting things, but it did feel so great to have such a good laugh.

Sylvia, 35, Kent, England

$\mathcal{S}$ometimes Mother substituted for the music teacher in our school. We were attending a so-called "progressive" school at the time, where children were encouraged to express their feelings.

Once, a group of children were sitting in a circle during music class with their arms on each other's shoulders, and they did not like what Mother was teaching them: They swayed back and forth and in unison sang, "We are bored, we are bored."

My mother's ideas about the advantages of a progressive education changed, and the next year we were sent to a different school.

Evie, 67, Burlington, Vermont

$\mathcal{M}$om has had Alzheimer's disease for a while now, and though it mostly saddens me to see my mother so weak, confused, and not herself, sometimes I just have to laugh at what comes up. For example, the other day she saw me coming down the hall at the nursing home and called out, "Hello, Mom!" I gently reminded her that I was her daughter, not her mother. Then I stayed for our usual visit.

When I came back the next day, Mom said to me, "You know, my mother was here yesterday, and I have to tell you, I really hated her haircut."

Katherine, 53, Appleton, Wisconsin

When I was a little boy, my mom would make up a story for me every night before I went to bed. I loved this routine, which always began with me asking, "Who did you see on the train today?"

Mom, who took the train to work, dreamed up some strange or exotic passenger. There was the man with hundreds of balloons, all blown up, in every shape, size, and color—and he would give one to anyone who asked. There was the man with a big mustache and sunglasses, whose suitcase, it turned out, was full of snakes! My favorite was about a briefcase attached to the wrist of a man who turned out to be a spy named "Ace Fly Delta."

At the end of every story, I'd ask: "Mommy, did that really happen?" and she'd say, "No, Sam, it didn't. But it made a good story, didn't it?" And I'd say, "Yup!"

Sam, 12, Boston, Massachusetts

$\mathcal{M}$y mother died when I was ten, so I went to live with my aunt, uncle, and cousins. My aunt was my substitute mother. Aunt Anni was a Bosnian immigrant in her twenties, still learning the ways of her new country and language, and the ropes of motherhood. I helped her with my young cousins, and she was there for me when I needed to talk about Mom.

Over the years, Aunt Anni made sure I had clothes, friends, birthday parties, a good education, and a place I could call home. She was also the one to listen to my daily triumphs or agonies. Coming from a faraway and war-torn country, my aunt had a different perspective on my life: She could tell me what was worth worrying about and what was not. Blowing a math test was bad; not having a boyfriend was not. Losing a girlfriend was sad, but sometimes could be resolved; giving in to peer pressure—the worst. She spoke frankly, earnestly, never lecturing, and always with love.

Betsy, 19, North Saint Paul, Minnesota

When my children were nine and eleven years old, they started going to visit my mother by themselves, for two weeks every summer. It was a two-hour airplane trip away.

A few days before they were due to leave, a big care package would always arrive in the mail. Mom would have sent the children chocolates, gum, books, little games, and all kinds of treats and toys, to help them get through the flight. Some might say Mom "spoiled" them. I just saw the love.

Emma, 68, Fort Worth, Texas

$\mathcal{M}$y mom has an incredible green thumb and loves to grow things, despite the fact that she lives in New York City. She's got a window box full of herbs right inside her kitchen window, herbs she uses a lot in her cooking. Her apartment is full of plants—both hanging and potted. In the summer, she keeps pots of tomatoes on the roof that are always juicy and ripe by August.

One time, when I was about five, Grandma sent Mom some French green bean seeds and we planted them in a discreet little space behind some bushes at the front of our building.

A few months later, we were walking home one rainy summer afternoon and she looked behind the bushes and exclaimed, "Oh my gosh! Will you look at these beans?! They're ready to harvest!" They were beautiful—slim and green and fresh with the rain. So there we were, soaking wet, picking green beans on lower Fifth Avenue.

Connie, 22, Manchester, New Hampshire

When I was in third grade and still living in New York City, I took acting on Saturdays. Mom and I would walk the mile to SoHo, where the acting lessons were, and on the way would look in the windows of stores with cool items like masks from New Guinea and doll furniture. Sometimes, we would buy birthday gifts for my brother and sister.

After the acting lessons, we would walk to a nearby deli and get some orange juice and some sesame bars, which to this day remind me of those Saturdays with my mom.

Emily, 14, Mishawaka, Indiana

*T*hanks to Mom, I discovered the joys of fishing. In the 1920s, our family went to a lakeside resort in northern Wisconsin for a short fishing vacation. My older brother was successful at age five (I was two). He caught three different types of fish, which he called "a bask, a pipe, and a porch" (bass, pike, and perch). This achievement, and his amusing malapropisms, became favorite family lore.

Back at the same resort a few years later, the jealous younger brother was eager for his chance. But I was scoreless—with only one day to go. Things were desperate, and Mom came to my rescue.

While Dad was fishing for the big muskies on a nearby lake, Mom saw a friend who had caught a large northern pike and persuaded him to hand it over. When Dad returned, he saw Mom proudly snapping photos of their younger son with a fish he could barely lift. My mother never "fessed up" and my many fisherman days ahead had begun.

Gordon, 82, Lake Forest, Illinois

$\mathcal{W}$hat is it the White Rabbit said? "I'm late, I'm late, for a very important date!" That is my mother. Or alternate with, *"You're* late, *you're* late, for ———!" (Fill in the blank: sports practice, CCD, school, karate, piano, walking the dog—you name it.)

Mom is always rushing, or imploring all or one of us four kids to hurry. She moves like a human windstorm and carries us along in her wake, while leaving the inside of our house a wreck, whenever she heads out the door. Once in the van, Mom's more composed, but then she's a driver on a mission, staying focused, beating yellow lights, and making phone calls to update our estimated time of arrival.

Genevieve, 14, Bethesda, Maryland

I was an only child, and my father was away on business for often weeks at a time. So, naturally, my mother and I spent a lot of time together and were wonderfully close. Almost like sisters, yet still mother and daughter.

Meanwhile, the war was advancing on Europe, and being Jewish, we needed to get out. Some close friends of my parents were going to America and we all could have gone with them, but my father would not leave. He did not want to start life in another country, and Mother would not leave him.

But Mother made the ultimate maternal sacrifice—she had me go. It took months to get all the legal documents for my departure, and while it was wrenchingly painful for both of us, it was worse for her. She could have had me stay with her, but she knew what was best.

I am now eighty years old and still living a full life. She and Papa died in a concentration camp.

Elisabeth, 80, Wilmette, Illinois

$\mathcal{M}$y dad had an insatiable lust for travel. Mom, who was content at home in her garden, gamely went on trip after trip—Dad would never have gone without her.

Down the Amazon, on African safari, swimming with seals in the Galápagos, exploring tombs in Egypt.... On the trips that we kids went on, it was Mom who shopped and packed and generally got us ready. Mom also provided the calm when plans went awry.

Once, in the New Guinea outback, my nine-year-old sister was sick and could not go with us on a bus trip to a small village. Mom, of course, stayed behind with her. We were at least four hours late coming back (the bus was too wide to turn around on the narrow road), and with no phone anywhere, Mom could only imagine the reason—though she bravely hid her fears from my sister.

As kids, we thought only Dad made the trips happen. As an adult, I'd like to belatedly salute my mom.

Louisa, 37, Edmonds, Washington

$\mathcal{M}$om and I were at the mall one Saturday, when we came across the now-immortal pink sweatshirt with the letters *C-O-O-L* in black across the front. It was summertime and I was struggling to learn how to ride my two-wheel bike.

Well, that afternoon we came home from the mall and, with my mom cheering me on from the kitchen window, I learned how to ride my bike. The most rewarding feeling was getting back in the car with Mom and going back to the mall to get that "COOL" sweatshirt, which I wore until the letters peeled off.

Tracee, 27, Mount Joy, Pennsylvania

$\mathscr{I}$n a suburb where most people drive most of the time, my mom walks. Or rides her bike. She'll drive if she has to, but otherwise it's walk or bike. It's kind of embarrassing, but then again I have to hand it to her for doing what she wants to do and for getting her exercise the way she likes.

Arielle, 13, San Jose, California

$\mathscr{M}$y mother is one of those passionate collectors of stuff from hotels and motels. In all the years that she's written me letters, she's never written letters on her own personal stationery. I've gotten letters on stationery from hotels, motels, and cruise ships, as well as postcards from the road. In fact, she sends me postcards from places she visited ten years ago, because she still has the postcards.

As for the soaps and the shampoos: When I visit her, she has a salad bowl full of soaps, shampoos, and conditioners from all the hotels she's been to, and whenever I shampoo, it's always from a bottle about two inches high.

Bobbie, 27, Frankfort, Kentucky

$\mathcal{M}$y mom has never been short on opinions. After a phone call or a day spent shopping together, my ears are ringing with her recent comments on contemporary life:

"They're going to ruin computers just like they did TV with all these advertisements!" and "Why are Americans in love with the Gap and Old Navy? Do we all want to dress the same, like the Communists in China?"

Mom's name is Jone, and Dad said that she should have a Jone Phone so people could call in for venting and advice. Jone fans, who would sport bracelets with WWJS (i.e., "What would Jone say?") would probably also agree with other Jonisms, like: "Why don't they have seats for customers in stores anymore? Don't they want people to be comfortable when they shop?" and "America would be a lot healthier if people stopped watching all the prescription ads on TV. Those just give people ideas on what might be wrong with them." Stay tuned.

Lindsay, 46, Minnetonka, Minnesota

$\mathscr{A}$side from the fact that Mom could not cook—her specialty was making "reservations"—Mom was the perfect fifties/sixties mother and wife. But the women's movement, along with Dad's bad temper, gradually changed her. When my brother and I were in high school, Mom got a job in an office—something I thought *so* embarrassing at the time, since none of my friends' mothers worked. She wasn't home when I came home from school either, which I didn't like. However, she always had a note on the counter—one for me and one for my brother, who would never tell me what Mom said. For me, the notes were usually words of encouragement or a quotation from some feminist who inspired her.

Those were hard years, but now I admire her courage for taking control of her life. She got Dad into counseling, which helped a lot, and seeing her so actively making changes and decisions that helped us all made me proud and happy to be her daughter.

Bindi, 41, Austin, Texas

$\mathcal{M}$y mother was renowned in our neighborhood for her cooking. The most delicious foods emanated from her kitchen, but there is one week I will never forget—the week of the cupcakes.

Since Mom was such a great cook, when my elementary school teacher asked for someone to volunteer a parent to bake cupcakes for our class party, I put up my hand. Little did I know that as I sat in my class raising my hand and volunteering Mom, other family members were doing the same thing.

One by one, we came home that day and told Mom how many cupcakes our teachers and the Scout leader wanted. Fortunately, Mom was a good sport and had plenty of stamina. She laughed and started baking.

In the end, there were cupcakes covering every surface of our apartment: the kitchen counters, the dining room table, dresser tops, even the top of the refrigerator—hundreds of beautiful chocolate cupcakes everywhere we looked. As always, Mom came through for us all!

Sheri, 49, Lake Buena Vista, Florida

$\mathcal{M}$y mother came from Arkansas, and her ancestors had written books on the Civil War, or, "The Waa between the States," as she always called it, in her gentle southern accent. I loved hearing Mother tell stories about her past and the distant past. She took an equal interest in my life, and the lives of my friends as well. All this made us as close as any mother and daughter could be, especially since I was an only child. Many of my friends were brought up by their nannies, not their parents. Sometimes, I'd come home and find a buddy who had come to see Mother for advice, or just to be in a loving environment.

Ginny, 68, Lake Forest, Illinois

$\mathcal{M}$y mother has loads of friends and loves talking with them. When I was little and we lived in Greenwich Village in New York City, we used to run into friends everywhere—the grocery store, at school, or just out for an errand. Nothing would be easier for Mom than to come to a halt and chat for what seemed like days, while my brother squirmed in his stroller and I stood by her side, waiting for the magic word *good-bye*. When we moved to the suburbs and were in the car more, still—at the grocery store, at school, or on an errand—Mom would see someone she knew and the inevitable chat time would follow.

Once, when we were at home and she was talking with a friend on the phone, I had an urgent homework question to ask her. "Wait until I've finished talking!" she said.

"But you're never finished!" I said, exasperated.

"You know—you're right," Mom said, and at least that time promptly got off the phone.

Allison, 17, Kalamazoo, Michigan

$\mathcal{M}$y children felt as if my mother was the "fun mother," while I had to provide the discipline. She would make cookies from scratch with them, and they would have cookie-dough fights—involving flour, eggs, sugar, etc.—a mess that never seemed to bother her. Mother would take them to the local cemetery and let them drive her car before they were allowed to drive, which I never knew until they were grown. She would serve breakfast to them on a bed tray with flowers and make the girls feel as if they were princesses. When she died, my children felt as if they had lost another mother.

Catherine, 68, Philadelphia, Pennsylvania

$\mathcal{I}$n Guyana, where we grew up, my mother went to visit her mother every weekend. She always took the same bus with the same driver—a Portuguese man who fell instantly in love with her. One weekend, my future father "kidnapped" her, taking her to his house, where he proposed—the beginning of a long, happy marriage.

Mommy never dated before she met Daddy, which maybe explains why she did not seem to understand why I enjoyed hanging out at the ice-cream stand or beach with my friends. If I stayed just a little too late talking, Mommy, angry and upset, would come find me—it was so embarrassing.

At age sixteen, I married the first man I fell in love with. My husband, five years older, was my teacher at school. I had twins at age eighteen and three more children by age twenty-three. My marriage lasted twenty-five hard years. I love my kids, but I wish my mother had advised waiting, and taking time to date, before marriage.

Claudette, 55, Atlanta, Georgia

$\mathcal{M}$y mom is an artist, mainly a children's portrait artist. Over the years, I have seen her paint portraits from either photos or live models. She's painted me three different times, at ages three and nine, and last year, before I left for college.

It always amazes me how she captures the one thing about a person that defines them. It might be something about a little girl's mouth or a little boy's eyebrows—just something I might not have noticed, except when Mom captures it, I think, "Yeah, that's it!" In my own portraits, she noticed things about me—a certain look in my eyes one year, a small dimple another—that I hadn't even seen in myself.

Alec, 19, Providence, Rhode Island

*A*bout twenty years ago, my parents started a school at the church they attended. The school started with a few lower grades and over the years was able to grow with its students to become a K–12 school. Throughout that time, and even after my parents' divorce, my mother served as the school's director and taught junior high school students.

In 2001, the school was able to start its first scholarship fund for needy students. The school board named the scholarship fund after my mother and held a ceremony to recognize her contributions. Mom then awarded the first scholarship.

I am so proud of the incredible legacy my mother has created. The gifts she has given the many students who have passed through the school's doors will far outlive her and will be reflected in the lives of the students. It is from her that I've learned the value of seeking ways to give of myself to others, and, in particular, to children.

Laura, 45, Houston, Texas

$\mathcal{M}$rs. Pincus was my "other mother" as I grew up. Her daughter, Debbie, and I were best friends, so I spent a lot of time at their house, usually around the kitchen table, which is ironic, because Mrs. Pincus was not a cook. But what she passed around that table was more nourishing than food.

What I remember best were the conversations. She, Debbie, and I would talk about everything. Mrs. Pincus listened to us and asked questions. At a time when we were forming our personalities and needed to be heard, she let us talk and paid attention. She thought we were wonderful.

We spent a lot of time laughing around that table. Mrs. Pincus had a great sense of humor, and one that appreciated my own. Her laugh was full, long, and heartfelt, and I loved the way her warm brown eyes looked at us with approval, the way she valued our company and made us feel worthwhile.

Anne, 45, Annapolis, Maryland

It was Saturday night years ago, and Alfred Hitchcock's film *Dial M for Murder* was on TV and my parents decided to have a family night watching this movie with us kids. It was intense and very riveting. The climax came when Grace Kelly, backed up against a desk in her house as her husband's hired assassin stalks her, grabs a pair of scissors off the desk.

At that point, Mom leaped up from the couch and blocked us from witnessing the brutal next move by spreading her dress out to cover the screen. My brother and I screamed bloody murder for her to move, but Mom held fast, and I didn't see it for myself until a few years ago.

Eddie, 33, Boulder, Colorado

$\mathcal{O}$ne winter afternoon, the afternoon of my fifth or sixth birthday, I went outside to play in the snow. As I made a little snowman, slid down the snowbank, and made snow angels, I could see Mom through the kitchen window. She wasn't always watching me, but she waved occasionally and was there the whole time I was out playing.

After dinner that night, Mom brought out the birthday cake. I was so amazed. "When did you make it?" I asked.

She said, "When you were outside playing." I felt so happy. Something about her seizing the moment when I went out, smiling and waving to me as I played and she mixed and baked, touched me deeply.

Marie, 43, Leyden, Massachusetts

$\mathcal{B}$ack in the thirties and forties, my mom was the glamour girl of the neighborhood. I thought she was too cool for words, and my friends *loved* her. Her style, clothes, and manner stood out, and one time some of her fairy dust even fell on me.

That was when Mom took my friend Anna and me to see Frank Sinatra at the Paramount Theater in New York City. It was 1943; Anna and I were eight years old, Mom twenty-nine—and Frank twenty-seven, and still just the backup act to Benny Goodman, but on the cusp of becoming the first teen idol. The theater was so packed, Anna and I had to share a seat. The crowd, mostly teenage girls, was delirious—just screaming as if hypnotized. We could barely hear Frank sing. It really was the first rock concert.

Naturally, after going, Anna and I had instant status in the neighborhood. As for Mom, seeing Frank Sinatra as if she were one of the girls just added to her legend.

Beverly, 67, Brooklyn, New York

Feliz cumpleaños!" I can hear my mother wishing me a happy birthday, either at my bedside as a child, or now, on the phone, first thing in the morning.

Mom, a Cuban immigrant, absolutely loves birthdays, and with six of us kids, plus Dad and herself, she's had plenty to celebrate. When I was young, each birthday was celebrated with a big family barbecue in our backyard, with all our aunts, uncles, and cousins. In Florida, even winter birthdays are celebrated outside, usually under a spectacular blue sky, with enormous white afternoon clouds.

The first time I asked Mom if I could have a birthday party with my school friends, she looked at me like I was crazy, but my aunts helped her understand American ways. Then she got totally into that, thinking up party themes, decorations, and games. She and I always made the cake together. Even now, I still come home to make the cake with her, and to celebrate with family and friends.

Cari, 24, Naples, Florida

$\mathcal{M}$y mom taught me the ten-year rule many years ago; I have lived by it and taught it to others ever since. The rule is, "If it won't matter in ten years, don't worry about it. If it will matter in ten years, then stand by it."

Mom said that rule guided her marriage. She let Dad make most of the daily decisions, since they wouldn't matter in ten years. But she would not budge when it came to deciding where to live and how many kids to have.

Every decision I make I run by the ten-year rule. I have three children and work full-time, but I've never missed a school play, dance recital, soccer practice, or class trip. I don't worry about what movie we see, where we go on vacation, and what trees get planted in the yard. Anyone who feels strongly about these things gets to decide.

Thanks to Mom's rule, I have been happily married for almost fifteen years.

Lisa, 42, Garden City, New York

$\mathcal{I}$n the early seventies, Mom went back to school to get her master's degree in library science. Every Monday night, she left Dad and the three of us to fend for ourselves, dinner being the main hurdle. Supermom that she was, and no doubt feeling extremely guilty about deserting us (her view) for the evening, Mom left us with a box of Hamburger Helper. So much for fending for ourselves!

These Monday nights resonate so clearly with my brother, sister, and me: that empty feeling caused by Mom's brief absences, and yet the pride in her efforts; the excitement of running free in the kitchen; and the horror of having to eat what we prepared (the tuna version comes to mind).

When Mom finally retired a few years ago after more than two decades as a junior high school librarian, we immediately knew how to honor her: with a box of Hamburger Helper.

Susan, 43, Corvalis, Oregon

*W*henever I was sick, Mom was there to make everything better. It didn't matter if I had the chicken pox, the flu, or any other ailment—Mom spent so much time making sure I had either food to eat (chicken soup), the right medicine, or a new game to play. Being sick was actually kind of fun because Mom was so good at taking care of me.

One time, my brother and I were both home sick and Mom let us play beauty parlor with her. We got to put curlers in her hair and do her makeup and she looked quite ridiculous when we were through, but she was so patient with us and it was so much fun.

To this day, one of my favorite games with my two girls is beauty parlor. I love to watch their faces as I get sillier and sillier looking, and I remember that day with my own mom.

Risa, 40, Nanuet, New York

$\mathcal{M}$y mother is not one to avoid the spotlight, but in this instance she would really have loved to. Back in the late sixties, Dad took Mom and us three kids to a big, garish dinner theater to see the comedienne Totie Fields. Totie, buxom, loud, and funny as a whip, was then in her heyday.

Several minutes into the show, Mom, who always had to go to the bathroom at the least opportune times, got up to go. As she passed the next table in the darkness, Totie, sensing a mark, interrupted her routine and yelled, "Put the lights on that lady!"

Like a deer trapped in the headlights, Mom stood bathed in the spotlight, mortified.

"And just where are you going, ma'am?" Totie inquisitioned at the top of her lungs.

Mom responded in a loud whisper, "I've got to pee."

After the gales of laughter died down, Totie delivered her final blow: "Well, lady, I've got to pee, too, but I can wait 'til my act is over!"

Ed, 49, Belmont, Massachusetts

$\mathcal{M}$y mother grew up on a farm in Wisconsin, one of seven children. Luxuries were hard to come by during her childhood, so the one frill that did come her way was something she never forgot:

On her fifth birthday, which fell on a May day, Mom, her brothers, sisters, aunts, uncles, and cousins held a picnic in an orchard not far from her house. For dessert, her aunt presented her with the most splendid birthday cake she'd ever seen. The cake was beautifully frosted, and on top of that were little chocolate-cream candies that had been cut up, just so, and laid out in a lovely design.

Years later, on a trip back to the farm, Mom pointed out to us the orchard where she had received this cake. And every year around Christmas, I search all over for, then send her, a box of her favorite chocolate-cream candies, to remind her of a cherished memory.

Colleen, 50, New Rochelle, New York

$\mathcal{M}$y mother was an only child. So was her mother, and even her mother's mother. Growing up, Mom always wished she could have a brother or sister to share her parents' attention. She also loved going to friends' houses and being among a bunch of brothers and sisters, even if they argued a lot. She made a promise to herself that she would never be a mother to an only child.

When Mom married and had a baby girl, it seemed like she was following in her mother's and grandmother's footsteps: My sister turned one . . . two . . . three . . . still no sibling. Suddenly (well, okay, after nine months), *boom!* I arrived, breaking not only the cycle of girls, but, more important, the cycle of only children, all in one. Thanks to Mom's promise to herself, and thanks also to Dad, I exist!

Andrew, 15, East Greenwich, Rhode Island

For my fortieth birthday, I decided to throw myself a small party at a restaurant. I invited my closest friends, and also my mom. I really wanted Mom to be there for this big event, but unfortunately Mom had long-standing plans to be out of town. It was disappointing, but I understood.

So what a surprise it was to walk into the restaurant that night and see Mom! She had canceled her plans and then called one of my friends to find out where the party was and when to show up. Good old Mom. She was my favorite birthday present that night.

Michelle, 42, Santa Monica, California

*M*y mom wanted to do something unusual to celebrate being "in her fifties." She did not want a big party with lots of friends but no time to visit with them all. So my brothers, sister, and I took over the plans for her and created what we considered Mom's ideal party.

The day dawned and Mom and Dad went, as instructed, to the bottom of a hiking path. Meeting them there were a dozen of Mom's closest friends. We served them all coffee and coffee cake, then the whole party went for a hike in the mountains. It took a few hours to reach the top, hours that Mom spent talking with friends and enjoying the fresh air and climb. When the group reached a certain flat stretch of land, we kids had prepared a rather unusual dinner party—with shrimp, chicken, bread, and wine served on a timber log by the edge of a wood.

Mom loved her birthday. So did Dad. So did her friends. I wonder what she'd like to do when she hits her sixties!

Marian, 23, Trondheim, Norway

$\mathcal{M}$y mother was not one for giving advice or opinions—I had three sisters for that. But sometimes a mother is the only person who can help, and so it was Mom whom I called for from my bedside one night, at age thirteen.

That afternoon, I had discovered that my closest friends had started smoking cigarettes. I had spent the past year or so begging my parents, heavy smokers each, to quit. Now, in the ladies' room of a movie theater, here I was accepting a cigarette myself! A friend helped me light it, and I took one uneasy puff and another. Then I looked in the mirror—and stubbed the cigarette out.

I told Mom what was bothering me, and she said calmly, "You have some really good friends, and they'll be your friends whether you smoke or not."

Mom was right, and I never troubled myself about cigarettes again. My wonderful girlfriends, with whom I'm still in touch, quit smoking about thirty years later.

Linda, 45, Washington, D.C.

$\mathcal{M}$ama was the hardest-working, most unusual woman I have ever known—a brilliant intellectual yet extremely provincial. Mama was born in a shtetl in Russia around 1900 (I'm not sure because she would never tell us how old she was). When she was still in her teens, she left home and was accepted as a female Jewish medical student, which was extremely rare, at the University of Odessa. There she met my father.

In 1917, when the revolution broke out, most students supported the Karensky government. But when the Bolsheviks took over instead, Stalin was in charge of executing all the students who might have supported Karensky's government. Through quick thinking and many miracles, my parents escaped. Mama never saw her parents again—they died at the hands of the Nazis.

Mama spent the rest of her life in America, which she loved with a passion. Even so, she lived with the nagging fear that someday, somehow, she would be sent back to Russia. Her fear ended with her death in 1978.

Elliott, 72, Lake Worth, Florida

$\mathscr{E}$very June, Ma would make an end-of-the-school-year cake. At first, my brother, Jake, and I were excited to see what kind of cake Ma had made and how she'd decorated it. But by middle school, and then high school, ugh! We began to dread the cake—it started this whole emotional drama with Ma, the cake meaning Jake and I were moving on ... even if it was only from seventh to eighth grade.

So while my brother and I celebrated the end of the year, it's fair to say Ma mourned. After a while, it became a joke. When Jake graduated high school, we said, "Ma, how about we make the cake for you?" We thought about making it as a bunch of little cakes—each in the shape of a tear.

Last year, when it was my turn to graduate, I said, "Ma, spare me the cake. You'll have to frost it in black. Let's go out for ice cream."

Danielle, 19, Gloucester, Massachusetts

On some school mornings when I just can't pull myself out of bed, Mom might say, "If you can get dressed, I'll take you to Stan's." Stan's is this great coffee shop, with the best hot chocolate and homemade muffins. That offer will get me out of bed fast and really start my day off right. Mom and I sit in our booth, Mom with her cappuccino and me with my usual, and slowly wake up before the school day begins.

Oliver, 10, Fulton, Georgia

$\mathcal{M}$om is an artist, and when I was an infant, she would bring me to her East Village studio while she worked. She made a portrait of us—me in the Moses basket, light streaming down from the skylight, while Mom contemplated her canvas.

When my sister was born, Mom and Dad decided we should move to the suburbs. There are no portraits of us or our life there. Mom was miserable.

One day, she took me and my sister to the city and found out she was pregnant. That night, I drew her a picture that looked like three-year-old scribble-scrabble, but I said, "Here, Mommy. This is us in New York City." She loved it, had it framed even, and says that picture inspired her to move us all back to the city. It had the energy and chaos that she missed.

A week after we moved into our loft, my brother was born. Mom's portrait of that time, bursting with color, still hangs in the living room.

Will, 24, Washington, D.C.

One day, I heard my mother shriek from upstairs. Something had just fallen from the sky and into our garden, and Mum ran out to see. Apparently, a baby mallard duck had fallen off its mother's back. It was only a couple of days old.

Mum let us keep the duck. We named her Tufty, and she became part of the family, along with our three dogs and two cats. Mum's only rule was that Tufty had to be carried around in one of Dad's socks when in the house.

Tufty was wonderful. She endeared herself to Mum so much that when Mum discovered Tufty making a not-so-hidden nest in her prized border flowers, she went along with Tufty's needs and pretended not to notice. Tufty laid four eggs that year, and she stayed with us four years. Mum seemed so caring about Tufty, I tried to convince her to take in a baby hedgehog I'd found—but there she drew the line.

Diana, 47, Hampshire, England

The evening of my thirtieth birthday, I spoke with my mother. I said, "Mom, I'm thirty years old, I haven't found a man that I want to settle down with; I have no children, I've been making art for twelve years with no acknowledgment or financial stability. I feel so unsuccessful. I'm afraid that at my age, I'll never succeed. I'm getting old. I'm really worried, Mom."

She said, "You have a roof over your head, clothes on your back, and food in your stomach. You are a success. Just keep on doing what you've been doing and you'll be all right. As far as getting old, you can't worry about that, because it's going to happen anyway. Don't waste the energy."

What Mom said seemed so simple, so abrupt, that I had to smile and laugh. I breathed a sigh of relief and said, "Thanks, Mom. You always say just the right thing. I love you."

Mom said, "I love you, too. Happy birthday, Leslie."

Leslie, 39, New York, New York

$\mathcal{C}$hristmas was a difficult time for my mother. All the festivities, decorations, and holiday gaiety were hard because it reminded her of the twenty-four-hour period when both of her parents died in a flu epidemic: Just before Christmas in 1916, when Mom was sixteen years old, Mom's mother went into the hospital with pneumonia. The next day, her dad went into another hospital and died. The next day, her mom died, not knowing her husband had passed on the day before. They were buried in a double funeral in a cemetery outside of Boston, and the local paper reported the whole sad tale.

Our family still celebrated Christmas—but when I was about nine years old, we started driving down to Florida, where the weather and scenery were so different that it blotted out the bad memories for Mom. Those "untraditional" Christmases created such happy memories for me that my husband and I made it a tradition with our kids to drive down to Florida for Christmas every year.

Dorothy, 76, Punta Gorda, Florida

*M*om, who was Episcopalian, was under a lot of pressure by her dad's parents to bring us kids up Catholic. This religious difference had been big enough between my two sets of grandparents that Mom and Dad had eloped, rather than choose a church to marry in. But when it came time to put us kids in Sunday school, they had to decide. Mom had made her decision from the start: Episcopal. And Dad was fine with that.

But it was a big deal to Dad's parents. My sister broke the news to Grandma and Gramps when they came to dinner that first Sunday. "We went to Sunday school at Holy Shepherd today!" she told them. With that, they knew that Mom had "won." There was no scene, but my grandparents went straight home.

A while later, Grandma called to say she had forgotten to tell Mom how much she liked our new drapes in the living room. It was her subtle way of saying, "Okay."

Fred, 38, Great Falls, Montana

*W*hen my mother was about twenty, she decided she wanted to go live in New York City. Her mother gave her $100 and wished her luck.

On her first day in the big city, Mom went straight to Rockefeller Center and said to the man in the employment office that she wanted to work there and that she'd do any job available. The man asked her if she'd been to college, and Mom said, "Yes, Bradford Junior College." Turned out, the man's daughter went there, and she and Mom had recently been bridesmaids in the same wedding together.

Mom got a job giving tours around Rockefeller Center and fifty-five years later can still give most of the spiel she used to say.

James, 50, Raleigh, North Carolina

$\mathcal{M}$y mom has reveled in her role as grandmother to ten grandchildren for almost twenty-five years now. When the first grandchild was on the way, just when the last of her four children got married, our backyard was promptly dug up and turned into a swimming pool.

Before long, Mom was hosting regular family reunions—making and serving three meals a day to kids, spouses, and many small grandchildren, for up to a week. Mom also loved having the grandchildren to herself and my dad for days at a time. To do this, Mom taught all her grandchildren good manners. She also taught each one to swim, over many summers, the years when they sported "Camp Mammy" T-shirts.

Though her grandchildren are mostly grown now, Mom still hosts a big reunion every summer. That's when Mom and Dad take their Christmas card picture, with all of us together, and the way she beams so proudly says it all.

Lucy, 51, North Scituate, Rhode Island

When I was young, Mom saw that I was creative and signed me up for Saturday art classes. Drawing, painting, cutting colored paper, the smell of glue, sculpting—I loved it.

At age seven, I did a portrait of my grandfather, which Mom framed and Grandpa hung over his workbench. I was proud to watch the white paper yellow over the years.

In college, I began as a business major—and was bored. With Mom's encouragement, I spent a semester in London, where I took an art history class—my turning point. The professor showed forty slides a day, explaining each artist's motivation, style, and influence. In the afternoon, I would ride my bike to the Tate or National Gallery and actually see these magnificent works of art. I was inspired to the max!

Ultimately, I melded business with art through my own photography studio. Even after twenty-five years, I still love going to work every day. And for Mom's support all along the way, I am eternally grateful.

Jim, 51, North Scituate, Rhode Island

$\mathcal{A}$ single childhood image of my mother stands out in my mind. Somehow, I know that she was thirty-one years old then, which means I was just five. She is standing by the kitchen sink, an apple-dappled apron tied around her waist. Her hair is dark brown, cut short above her ears with a pointy curl lifting over her forehead like a breaking wave, and I am looking up at her, the top of my head barely reaching the counter beside me. I gaze, thinking how beautiful she is, the most beautiful woman in the world.

Though I certainly haven't always perceived her that way since, and though now she is already seventy-six and I am almost fifty, I can still retrieve that frozen memory and feel the awe and unsurpassable love I felt at that random moment.

Susan, 49, Mount Kisco, New York

$\mathcal{M}$om has assembled scrapbooks all her life. Her books contain the highlights of all of our lives and I love to look at the albums whenever I visit. There's Mom and Dad's wedding, there's me as a baby, and then my two brothers at each of their births. My brothers and I also have our own albums, now yellowed with age. Inside are newspaper clippings, pictures, photos, and birthday cards, like time capsule items representing other eras, from infancy through college. I like looking at my brothers' albums to remember highlights of their lives and to see what events of theirs I missed.

Then there are Mom's seven grandchildren, ranging in age from ten to nineteen: Each one has at least two thick photo albums of his or her own, marking first steps, birthdays, school plays, vacations, graduations. Many pages have captions that Mom has clipped from magazines to go with the pictures. She puts so much care into each page, just as she cares about each one of us.

Ann, 50, Kansas City, Missouri

$\mathcal{S}$pending two weeks in Maine every summer is a family tradition that my mom has made sure we carry on. My great-grandparents and their family started it. Then my grandma and her family continued it. It was easy for them, since they lived not far from there, in Boston. But for Mom and our family, it's a bit more complicated, since we live in Ohio. It involves lots of planning, taking planes, and renting cars. . . .

Still, Mom feels strongly about continuing the Maine tradition, and I've gone back there every summer of my life. I love hearing stories about Mom and Grandma and even my great-grandmother, when they were my age and walking down the same old roads or going to the same lobster restaurant or beach. Vacation in Maine is always fun, but knowing the link to our family's past makes it all the more meaningful, and I'm glad Mom has made the effort for us to do that.

Jessica, 19, Oxford, Ohio

$\mathcal{M}$om's never had a hard time keeping in touch. She always writes thank-you notes, plans birthday cards to arrive on time, has Christmas planned out well before Halloween. And though I live in Illinois and Mom in Florida, she's been present for all my important milestones—the birth of my children, my fortieth birthday, graduations, and many times in between. She just knows when to come and always brings so much good cheer and joy.

Gail, 52, Naperville, Illinois

$\mathcal{I}$ was ten when I found out Mom had cancer. Mom said that she'd had it before and expected to get better this time, too. Mom then told me that she was going to get her hair cut very short, because soon it would start to fall out and it would be less noticeable if it were already short. I asked if I could come with her when she got her hair cut, and she said we could spend the whole afternoon together.

We went to the hair salon, then to Central Park, and had a wonderful day. Back at our building, we rode up the elevator with a neighbor, who exclaimed, "Oh, Maddie—I love your new haircut!"

Mom thanked her and smiled but did not look at me to share our secret. That was when I really understood that Mom was sick. She died seven months later.

Anthony, 20, New York, New York

$\mathscr{M}$y mother suffered from Alzheimer's disease for seven years, during which time I was married with three young children. It was a struggle to share this wondrous part of my life with her, but I never stopped trying.

This year, Mom seemed worse than ever when I went to see her before Hanukkah. When I came home, I had my children call her to wish her a happy holiday. Then I got on the phone.

"Mom, those were your *grandchildren!*" I said.

She seemed confused and then—for one miraculous moment—her mind cleared. "My grandchildren?" she asked.

"Yes, Mom."

"Oh Debbie, I hope you are enjoying them."

"Oh yes, Mom!" I took a breath and asked, "Did you enjoy having your children?"

"Oh yes. I enjoyed my children so much."

Those were her last words to me. She then faded into a deep sleep and died by morning. I will always treasure our last conversation.

Debbie, 45, Larchmont, New York

Every summer of my childhood, my mother, sister, and I would take the overnight train from New York to Indianapolis to visit my grandmother. My mother and grandmother were Polish immigrants, and getting together was not taken for granted.

Our four-week stay began with tears, cries of joy, and lengthy hugs between Mom and Grandma, who spoke to each other (between sobs) in Yiddish, the only time I heard Mom speak anything but English. There was never a happier household than that first night at Grandma's. On those trips, Mom was more her mother's happy little girl than a mother herself.

As each vacation came to an end, Mom would get a sad look in her eyes. There would be sudden tears and a sort of panic in the air as Mom prepared to leave her mother for another year. It would be a long time until my mother finished her grieving.

Deborah, 40, King of Prussia, Pennsylvania

$\mathcal{M}$y mom was loving and in many, many ways a great mother—but I always felt she was hiding something from me. There was the locked bedroom door at odd times, her cheek quickly turned away from a kiss, the way she sat away from us at the beach....

Another thing—Mom was always perfectly dressed, her face carefully made up and with a thick layer of foundation.

At age thirty-nine, I found out that the secrets and the makeup were hiding something that, to her, was deeply shameful: Mom had a wine spot on her face.

Mom told me this right before going in for laser surgery to have it removed. But even then she wouldn't show me.

When I finally saw my mom without makeup, it was shortly before she died. Though the laser surgery had failed, her skin was flawless, having hardly seen the light of day in decades, and the wine spot—after all her covering up—was barely worth noting.

Rebecca, 44, Montclair, New Jersey

*M*y family is French—and *Maman* is the best cook in the world. I can say that because we have lived all over the world—in Russia, Azerbaijan, the Ivory Coast, Mexico, and the United States. I have eaten feasts and wonderful dishes everywhere, but I still prefer *Maman*'s meals. In tiny, dark kitchens, in rental houses with ancient stoves or rustic ovens, *Maman* has still produced our favorite family recipes, including crepes every Sunday and *galette aux fraises* (a strawberry pastry). My father's job requires us to move every few years, so I appreciate that my mother, through her cooking, can bring the taste and feel of home to us each night at the dinner table.

Claudine, 16, Victoria, British Columbia, Canada

$\mathscr{I}$ never wanted to go to my mother's alma mater—a women's college. Reluctantly, I applied and begrudgingly I accepted. But while I was there, I began to see the advantages of going to the same college as my mother. Mom knew all the traditions and also understood the experience of being a northerner in a southern setting. When I talked with her on the phone, she really knew what I was talking about and could picture my classrooms, the walk across campus, my life in the dorm. It was so much fun going through all this with Mom.

Years have passed since then. Now we share reunions—at my twentieth and her forty-fifth, we got together with mutual friends. This year, at my twenty-fifth and her fiftieth, we plan on spending extra time together. It's an understanding not too many women can share.

Irene, 47, Joliet, Illinois

$\mathcal{M}$y parents were at a cocktail party and one of the guests asked my mother if she had any children. My mother said yes and the guest asked, "How many do you have?"

"Six," my mother replied, smiling politely.

The guest was appalled. "Six! How can you hope to educate them all?"

Continuing to smile, my mother answered, "We're hoping some of them are stupid."

Andrea, 42, New York, New York

$\mathcal{I}$ loved to go to the beauty shop when Mom was working, to watch her in her white uniform, looking so smart. Her hair, teased high on top and swept back on the sides, with a hint of bangs in front, was lacquered to perfection, not a strand out of place, and she wore frosted orange lipstick and false eyelashes, always the most beautiful operator in the place. They were all called "operators," those hairdressers, and their productivity was measured in "heads."

If Mom came home saying, "I did twenty-one heads today," I knew that she was exhausted and that her pockets were crowded with tips that she'd count out on the kitchen table the next morning, rolling quarters, adding totals, noting amounts in her special work calendar, commenting on especially cheap or especially generous customers. Regular customers were called steadies and were identified by the amount of their usual tip, amounts that grew larger over the years, eventually measured in dollars rather than quarters and dimes.

Mary Ann, 31, Brooklyn, New York

*M*om grew up in northern England in a quiet, proper household of the 1950s. Order reigned in this small industrial town. The laundry pegged perfectly on the line, the roast—a tiny lamb roast—for Sunday dinner that her mother made last until Tuesday.

Mom burst out of that life as soon as she could. She came to New York in 1968 "on a visit" and never left. The East Village, where she settled, was the opposite of her early life: full of art and artists, nutty bohemians, dancers, writers, spontaneous parades, and people exploring life without limits (for better or worse). And the deli sandwiches! Sandwiches larger than the Sunday roast—and that was for four people and three meals! She still talks about the deli sandwiches.

Mom has made her way *her* way. She works hard as a lawyer but makes sure I don't miss the things she did: gardening in a communal garden, dressing up at Halloween, and finding joy in unexpected things.

Rachel, 15, New York, New York

When I was little, dreams scared me. Even good dreams. Mom and I agreed that the best dream was no dream at all. So she helped figure out a bedtime routine perfectly designed to help me sleep happily through the night.

First, Mom read me a story. When that was over, she took a tiny little Piglet charm that had come off a necklace and placed it under the lamplight and said, "Piglet, if any dreams come into Emma's room tonight, blow them out like this."

Then Mom would proceed to puff into Piglet's miniature ear, and then my ear, eight times—one for each kind of dream Piglet was supposed to blow away—always listed in this order: sleepy, good, bad, alien, weird, gross, scary, and annoying.

To this day, whenever I have trouble getting to sleep, I think back to Mom and Piglet, and before I know it, I'm sound asleep.

Emma, 15, Arlington, Texas

*M*y mother, who does not care for cooking, long ago figured out how to avoid the job of peeling hard-boiled eggs for the traditional Passover seder. This ceremonial dinner requires everyone at the table—family, grandparents, aunts, uncles, and cousins—to take what is supposed to be a perfectly peeled hard-boiled egg. But the way we've always done it is for everyone to take a hard-boiled egg in the shell, then the whole table has a contest to see who can peel theirs the fastest (I always thought this was the way everyone did it).

One year, however, we all took our eggs and began cracking them on our plates, only to discover that Mom had forgotten to hard-boil them! Whoops.

Susanne, 11, Los Angeles, California

When I was a little girl, I lived with my parents, brother, and sister in a brownstone house on the Upper East Side of New York City. My father went to work every day in a dark tweed coat, gray hat, and briefcase. Mother stayed home to manage the house, and we children went to school and played in Central Park afterward.

When Daddy and Mother went out in the evening, Mother would put on a pretty dress and come to our bedroom to say good night and hear our prayers. When she leaned over my bed to kiss me, I thought she was the most beautiful person in the world.

Mary, 71, New Canaan, Connecticut

$\mathcal{M}$y mom just turned fifty. I didn't realize a grandma could be so young, but lucky for me that she is. Otherwise, how would she have the energy to chase after my two-year-old daughter and make her giggle, or take her out to eat and keep her entertained, or shop for all of those toys and cute outfits that she buys for her?

A girl couldn't ask for a better grandma than my mom. I tell my daughter all the time how much better our lives are because her grandma and grandpa live right up the road. They help us out and visit us and provide our family with a never-ending source of love and laughter.

Sheila, 25, Mobile, Alabama

$\mathcal{M}$y mother, an actress on Broadway before she married Daddy, loved music and played the piano. We children stood around her and one of us turned the pages. We learned to sing many songs. She was also very good at taking our favorite stories and setting them to music.

Once, she put the story of *Ferdinand the Bull* to music: During the bullfight scene, she chose music from *Carmen;* when Ferdinand was sent back home because he wouldn't fight, Mother chose the "Going Home" theme from Dvořák's *New World* symphony. Another favorite was her "Night before Christmas." How we loved to hear these stories.

Mother took us to the Metropolitan Opera, where we saw *Hansel and Gretel* and other operas. We had to listen several times to the recording of an opera on the Victrola at home before we were allowed to see it.

Love of music was passed on to her children—and to her grandchildren. The apple does not fall very far from the tree.

Eve, 70, Tulsa, Oklahoma

*B*efore we left for school every morning, Mom would usually tell my sister, Arlene, and me what she was serving for dinner. If it was something we liked, our mouths would water all day in anticipation. If it was something we disliked, like liver and onions, we talked about running away from home.

However, we had always been taught to eat without complaint whatever was put in front of us. So we ate.

There was a meal Mom made occasionally that Arlene and I disliked intensely. Since Mom and Dad were trying to save money, we figured Mom made this meal to cut costs. She would sauté some onions in a frying pan and then pour in a drained can of peas. After the peas had heated for a while, she would break some eggs over the peas, put on a cover, and let the eggs cook. Yechh!

Many years later, Mom mentioned that Dad actually liked eggs and peas and was surprised to hear that Arlene and I felt otherwise.

Carol, 50, Grahamsville, New York

When I started dating, my mom asked to sit down and talk with me. She discussed trust and respect. She told me she understood the hormones that were raging inside me.

"Remember where you come from," she added.

It was a very poignant discussion, a true mother-and-daughter talk. But I was quite startled when she said, "Just remember—you can do anything you want with a boy . . . . ," then added quickly and emphatically, "from the neck up."

Eva, 58, Teaneck, New Jersey

$\mathcal{M}$y parents are both from small towns in Kansas, which is what attracted them to the life of overseas diplomats. Dad worked at the embassy, while Mom put on the parties. My brother and I were technically American, but growing up first in Japan, then in Africa, for our first dozen or so years, we didn't feel like anything. Dad didn't really understand why that bothered me so much, but Mom did.

In Nairobi, whenever possible, Mom would somehow find me the latest American teen magazine or, even better, a *TV Guide*. How I longed to watch shows like *Batman* and *Gidget*! Mom acted out whole episodes of *I Love Lucy*, which made me laugh so hard. I can also remember long, hot afternoons with Mom telling me bits and pieces of her childhood or describing wonders of America, like the Grand Canyon and New York City.

Dad was transferred to the States when I was fifteen, and thanks to Mom, it was like greeting an old friend.

Elizabeth, 45, Chatsworth, California

$\mathcal{I}$n the pre-women's-movement world of the late fifties, most women were discouraged from breast-feeding. They were told it wasn't as healthy for the baby as formula, that it certainly was not as proper as a bottle when in public, and just not worth the trouble and extra fatigue for the mother.

My mother and her best friend had babies about the same time and vehemently disagreed with all the accepted notions of the day. They both wanted to breast-feed and both did, despite the doubts voiced by Dad (now apologetic) and the objections voiced by my grandmother, not to mention society in general. To bolster their determination, Mom and Aunt Nora would call each other on the phone at least once or twice a day, cheering each other on.

Allie, 42, Beaver Creek, Ohio

Amazing and Wonderful Things about My Mom (Part 2)

She didn't kill me when I was a teenager. She bought awful clothes when I wanted them and beautiful clothes to remind me of my own inner elegance. She loves animals. She let me be a tomboy. She could do amazing dances to South Pacific drum music. She did 900 million loads of laundry. She made dinner every night, thousands of times. She created the best birthday cakes. She taught us good manners. She has forgiven me for all the rotten things I said and did. She let us have pet alligators, rabbits, snakes, and a raccoon. She has given endlessly to her community. She helped bring the AIDS project in Boulder to fruition. She worked to give rape victims a safe place to recover. She helped women understand their right to choose. She bought us a trampoline. She took care of me when I had my babies. She's good to my husband. She adores her grandchildren. I am proud she is my mother. I am proud to be her daughter.

Jeannie, 41, Bend, Oregon

Dad's maxims:

1. Be true to yourself.

2. Never lend or borrow money.

3. Learn something new every single day.

4. Never break a promise.

5. Always be a sport.

Mom's maxim:

1. Never leave the house without makeup. People will judge you by your looks and the clothes you wear.

All my life I valued the things my father said. In retrospect, however, Mom's maxim was not as superficial as I thought.

Butchie, 32, Hot Springs, Arkansas

I am still grateful for the time my mother saved my twin sister and me from extreme embarrassment. We were about seven years old and having a grand old time hiding and giggling under the white-linen–covered tables at our parents' formal summer garden party. But when we almost tipped a whole platter of food onto the ground, we were unceremoniously sent up to our room to amuse ourselves and told to keep out of trouble.

Instead, a boisterous game of "panty throwing" ensued, and since it was a warm summer's evening, our bedroom window was wide open. Out sailed a pair of white frilly lingerie (embellished with tiny pink rosebuds!), which landed "plop" into a glass of beer held by one of my father's business associates. Picking the dripping article out of his drink, the man looked up at the window and called out, "Do these belong to anyone?" to which my mother replied, "Yes, they're mine. And they *were* clean!"

Maddie, 42, Faringdon, England

$\mathcal{O}$ne of our simplest yet fondest memories is a tradition from our mom, which we have passed on to our children. Every night, my mom would "tuckle" in all of us. She would go from room to room and would ask if we wanted to be "tuckled in," which meant she would tuck the covers snug around us like mummies. We loved it, and if for some reason she forgot to ask, you would surely hear a little voice coming from one of our bedrooms, saying, "Mommy? Will you tuckle me in, please?"

It was a feeling of comfort and security we will always hold close to our hearts. Simple yet meaningful.

Jill, 45, Lynn, 43, Janice, 41, and Paul, 39, Monroe, Connecticut

*O*ur family moved when I was in third grade, and I had to change schools. I was shy and insecure at school, but I came up with a plan that helped me feel strong throughout the day:

I would wake up a little early, before my mother came in my room. I would then go into my parents' room, where they were still asleep, and crawl into bed next to my mother. I would watch her body as she breathed and put myself on the same inhalation-exhalation pattern. I was convinced that we would be breathing in unison for the rest of the day.

Whenever I felt shy or insecure at school, I would remember that my mom and I were on the breathing schedule and I would feel much more confident.

Amy, 45, Allen, Texas

When Mom found out I was in labor with my first child, she came to New York City to be with me and my husband, Paul. I was still at the hospital when she arrived, which was about three A.M., and I begged her to go to our apartment, which was nearby and lots more comfortable. Mom agreed and Paul put her in a cab, telling the driver, "Greenwich Avenue."

Unfortunately, Mom ended up on "Greenwich Street," which was quite far away, a mistake Mom didn't realize until too late. So Mom walked along the dark, empty streets of SoHo until she found two men standing on a corner. Mom thought to herself, "Those men are some women's babies." Inspired by that idea, she went up to them and explained that she was lost. The men kindly escorted her all the way home, though it took her years before she told me.

Philippa, 38, San Rafael, California

$\mathcal{M}$y mother brought into my life a sense of elegance, aesthetics, and savoir faire. She is the epitome of elegance. It is in her demeanor, in the way she dresses, in the way she places her flowers, in the way she sits down, and in her beauty.

I remember a New Year's Eve. I was five years old and she came down the stairs. I felt there was this cloud of tulle and black-and-green satin floating toward me and enveloping me. I think we all gasped. She kept this up all her life, never a hair out of place, even in the times she was depressed.

She is ninety-two years old and even today she is graceful and elegant. It is a pleasure to watch her.

Mariuccia, 56, Belize City, Belize

$\mathcal{M}$y mother was nurse, an R.N., during the depression. She was a single mom with two young boys, and we all lived with my grandmother. Mom worked long hours, and though I didn't get to see her very much, she loved being a nurse.

So when I think of my mom, I think back to being a little boy, watching her in the living room as she got ready to go to work. The ironing board would be out, and there would be the smell of fresh clothes in the air, since she always wore a freshly pressed uniform. Likewise, her white shoes would be freshly polished. She always wore her nurse's pin, and she was so proud of that. Sometimes, this was all I saw of her for that day. Even our dog knew the routine—once Mom put on her uniform, that meant no going in her car. Too soon, off she would go in our brown Studebaker, and Grandma would get us ready for school.

Jackson, 72, New York, New York

When I was little, probably about five years old, I kept seeing commercials on TV for some restaurant's all-you-can-eat ribs special. At the very end of the commercial, there was a man eating shrimp. I confused ribs and shrimp. I kept begging my mom to take me there because I wanted ribs (or so I thought). We finally went and I asked for ribs. But when my meal came, and it was a big plate of drippy brown meat instead of pretty little pink shrimp, I started crying hysterically and saying, "But I want ribs!" over and over again. I couldn't explain that I really wanted shrimp because I didn't know the word.

Anyway, there was no calming me down, so Mom let me have a sip of her strawberry daiquiri. Next thing she knew, I had downed the entire thing. Hey, at least it kept me quiet.

Reese, 21, West Valley City, Utah

was the middle child and only boy of six kids. When I was ten years old, my two older sisters were sixteen and fourteen, and my younger ones were five (twins) and two. In my mind, I had a "waste of siblings"—all those bodies and not one to play basketball with.

One afternoon, I was sitting around, when Mom came up and asked if I'd like to shoot some "hoops." I didn't even know she knew the term! I said okay, and we went out to the driveway to play. She was amazing! High school varsity, she said. I had no idea. Even the twins watched, in awe. Who knew Mom could do anything so "unmomlike"? When the baby woke up from her nap, Mom had my older sister baby-sit while she took me to Baskin-Robbins. She had a Jamoca almond fudge sundae, and I had a double scoop of bubblegum and coconut. I still savor the memory of that afternoon.

Adam, 19, Baltimore, Maryland

$\mathcal{M}$y mother was a suffragette as a young woman. She felt ardently about political issues. When President Roosevelt was running for his second term as president, our parents didn't agree on whom to vote for. My father wanted Roosevelt to win and my mother wanted Landon to win. I agreed with my mother, since her influence was so strong, and I went to school chanting, "Vote for Landon, vote for Knox—Roosevelt has the chicken pox!" That seemed to me to settle the matter, though voters were to think differently and elected Roosevelt by a landslide.

Nevertheless, Daddy was absentminded and forgot to register in time to vote. My mother didn't remind him. So when Election Day came, Mother said he locked her in the apartment all day and wouldn't let her vote.

My political allegiance shifted to the Democrats as I grew older. If my mother knew, she might say, "Well, at least you had the sense to marry a Republican."

Ann, 72, Lake Forest, Illinois

*D*o you remember driving Keri and me to Gram's on your way to work and stopping at McDonald's so that we could get our apple-and-cheese Danish? I do. I knew you loved us then because you made sure we were well fed, and we knew that someone who loved us was going to take care of us.

Do you remember calling poison control after you found out I drank from the plant spritzer? Thank you for being calm and making sure I "didn't die." Do you remember the time I broke my wrist and we went the whole weekend without knowing? I remember how bad you felt when you found out it was broken. I knew how much you loved me then.

Do you remember always buying rice pudding and a treat, probably a miniature, at the Pepperidge Farm store in the Kmart plaza after dentist visits? A good mom takes her kids to the dentist. A great mom takes away the pain of a cavity. Do you remember a call from Camp Berger to come and pick me up early? Thank you for coming, even though it was against the advice of others. I knew then how much you loved me. Do you remember a similar call from Boston? Thank you again. Do you remember you told me that you thought I was beautiful and I told you, "You're my mom, you're supposed to say that"? I realize now that not all moms say that. Thanks for saying I'm beautiful.

Do you remember when I called you to tell you I was engaged? As soon as I heard your voice, I couldn't stop crying. I knew then how much I loved you.

Some people say with dread, "I'm turning into my mother." I would be proud to one day say that I am even half the mother, wife, and woman that you are.

Tera, 29, Plainville, Connecticut

*A*fter a heavy snowstorm, which left huge icicles hanging from our roof, I was shoveling the front walk, thinking about hanging out with my friends, who were on their way over.

From inside, Mom came to the door and said, "Bill, can you please shovel the icicles off the roof over the door?"

"Can't I do it later?" I asked.

"No, do it now or you'll never get to it," Mom said firmly.

"Fine," I agreed. So I went upstairs with my shovel, opened the window, went out on the little roof over the door, and proceeded to shovel off the snow. Just then, my friends arrived. Their shouts knocked me off balance and I went sliding down the roof and landed on my back in front of the house.

"Come quick!" they called to my mom. "Bill's fallen!"

Mom came running out. "What happened?"

"I was shoveling and fell off the roof," I said.

I'll never forget her response: "And just what were you doing on the roof?"

Bill, 30, Philadelphia, Pennsylvania

$\mathcal{M}$y mom was artsy and offbeat compared to most mothers I knew. True, she wore a uniform as my Girl Scout troop leader, but she'd wear bright yellow patent leather shoes with it.

Before she married, Mom was a professional calligrapher and met Dad while she was working for a well-known package designer. Calligraphy took a backseat while raising six kids, but her creativity seeped in right along with necessity.

Mom's "day" began once we kids were asleep. It was then she'd head off to her fabrics and patterns and sewing machine. For Halloween, Mom would make professional-looking, all-lined costumes: Lions, pandas, and clowns come to mind. One year, our Easter outfits were sleeveless dresses with tiered chiffon skirts—one sister in yellow, one sister in aqua, while my brothers were coordinated in suits.

I never saw Mom making any of these things. It was like magic to me: They just appeared. But now I know why it was Dad who served us breakfast every morning, while Mom slept.

Meg, 43, Burlington, Vermont

$\mathcal{M}$y mother's philosophy toward mealtimes was "Make (or buy) it simple." Spaghetti, pizza, chicken, whatever was easiest.

That approach made Jewish holidays stand out as if illuminated in spotlights. For Jewish holidays, Mom would pull out all the stops: Tablecloths, good silverware, and china came out of cupboards, and fresh flowers were in vases everywhere. Delicious smells would emanate from the kitchen at least two days before any special occasion. Mom would be busy baking the recipes passed down to her from her mother, and she would be following them exactly. At some point, Mom started teaching me the recipes so I could do the same someday.

It is now that "someday." I have children and a husband, though Mom has passed away. Like her, I keep meals simple, except for the Jewish holidays. Then out come the tablecloths, silverware, china, fresh flowers, and special family recipes. I see that it's all such a gift—to myself and my family—and a tribute to Mom, who would have been proud.

Alysa, 45, Larchmont, New York

At the beginning of every school year, my mother, Mrs. Clark, would take five of us kids to the local shoe store to buy five pairs of Catholic school regulation oxfords. One year, as we all came through the door, the salesman looked at my mother and said, "Hello, there, Mrs. Lewis."

My mother sized him up. "Have you taken a memory course?" she asked.

"Why, yes!" he said. "How did you know?"

Deadpan, she answered, "Because I'm the other half of the expedition."

Andrea, 42, New York, New York

$\mathcal{I}$ remember when I saw the movie *Stepmom* with my mother. In one scene, the dying mom confronts the young stepmom and reveals that underneath her hatred for the stepmom is the fear that she won't be able to see her daughter get married and she won't be missed.

I remember looking over at my mom at that moment in the movie theater and being overwhelmed by gratitude for her loving presence in all of the most important events of my life, from my own birth to the birth of my daughters.

Our family is so close that it's easy to take the people in it for granted. But I know many women who don't have mothers, or any women, for that matter, whom they can count on for unconditional love and support. Simply put, I am what I am because of the ideals my mother has taught me, the advantages she has given me, and the love she has shown me through my whole life.

Barbara, 31, Lincoln, Nebraska

When I was four years old, Mom let me become a preschool dropout. Though I'd loved preschool when I was three, that fall I started withdrawing from the class and crying for Mom to take me home. Being so young, I couldn't explain to Mom or Dad why I was behaving this way. Mom suspected it had something to do with my brother being two years old and finally becoming something of a person. Mom would tell my older sister and me about his play dates and the things he did all day—and I think I just wanted to be with him and not in school.

So Mom let me drop out, and it was just what I wanted. We played with my brother's friends in the morning and came back to the apartment for lunch. My brother and I would then change into our bathing suits, the better to run around, play, and jump on Mom and Dad's bed. It was one of the most wonderful, free years of my life.

Alice, 13, New York, New York

$\mathcal{M}$y stepmother, Anna, grew up in Hampstead Heath, a London suburb, where she had a "proper" upbringing. She learned things through strict teachers, books, and long, rainy walks in the country. At first, it seemed like every sentence of hers had the word *tradition* in it.

Anna and my dad met on an airplane from London to New York, and she ended up marrying him and moving to Saint Louis, where we lived, when my brothers and I were eight, ten, and almost twelve. I can only imagine how chaotic our life seemed to her, after we had been living with a bachelor dad for three years. By then, our "traditions" were hard and fast, though, unlike hers, they consisted of racing through our homework, watching regular TV shows, blowing our allowance on candy and comic books, and dinner with Dad at McDonald's every Friday night.

But Anna was cool. What I see now is that she loved my dad and, by extension, us—that what she saw was what she wanted, even if it took getting used to. It worked.

Pat, 30, Elgin, Illinois

his is a story of what someone does out of love: heartbreaking, difficult work. My mother suffered from severe depression the last six years of her life. My sister did not want to be bothered with family problems and Dad did not know how to deal with Mom's illness.

I have always been close with Mom. After things got rough, Mom moved nearby and sometimes stayed at our house during particularly difficult times. It was a balancing act then between having my very young kids be with their grandma and yet not wanting them to see her in a bad light. What I realize now is, my kids never saw the bad—Mom adored them and they adored her back. They still miss her. And they learned that when you love someone, you take care of her.

When Mom died, I felt that I had done everything I could for her. Peace of mind and the love I still feel for Mom are a great reward.

Lisa, 45, Manchester, Connecticut

I grew up in South Africa during the sixties and seventies, when a posh British colonial lifestyle was still the norm for those of us with English roots. My father was a world-renowned medical specialist and my mother ran our house with a staff of maids and servants. Mum and Dad were extremely social, but deep down, I think my mother was bored, which made her feel tired.

Perhaps that is why Mum would say to me every day, and I mean e-v-e-r-y day, when I came home from school, "I'm going up to rest. Even if the queen of England phones and invites me to tea, you're not to wake me up."

Mum now lives in New York City, where life is so stimulating, she no longer naps at all. But I'm in the suburbs with three young children and seize any opportunity for an afternoon nap, which I always preface with, "Even if the queen of England phones and invites me to tea, you're not to wake me up!"

Caryn, 35, Litchfield, Connecticut

$\mathcal{M}$y mother was a delightful portrait of contrasts: a southern lady with a drawer full of dainty gloves; a Labor Zionist who fought for the establishment of Israel; a mother who taught me the importance of a nicely set table; and a social activist who taught me the importance of fighting for justice, who had me march with her on the 1963 March on Washington.

A feminist before the word was invented, Mom came of age during the depression, and, as one of eight Orthodox Jewish children, was prepared to make her own way in the world. Widowed by age thirty, Mom taught business education to high schoolers and adults to support herself and child (and continued even after she married my dad).

Mom died just six weeks after my daughter was born. But my boys remember a grandma who always had candy and ice cream for them, who played cards like a riverboat gambler, and who always pressed a dollar in their hands for "walking-around money."

It's nice to think about her.

Marian, 52, Baltimore, Maryland

$\mathscr{M}$om is the supersensitive, artsy, and creative type, who just can't bear taking public transportation. Even as a struggling puppeteer (her first job), she could hardly afford cabs, but she took them anyway, including cabs to go visit her boyfriend (now Dad). Concerned about the expense, Dad showed her how to take a city bus, since she refused to take the subway.

Mom agreed that the bus was easy and much cheaper, and on her next visit she took the bus. Sitting in the back, Mom started listening to this old woman talk about how she and her husband had saved for their whole lives to go on vacation, and how the night before they were set to leave, her husband had a heart attack and died.

So moved by the sad story, Mom arrived at Dad's apartment sobbing and hardly able to talk. Dad thought she'd been mugged! When Mom finally calmed down enough to tell Dad what had happened, Dad sighed and said, "Better stick to taxis." And she has ever since.

Florence, 20, New York, New York

*T*he summer before sixth grade, I went to sleep-away camp, and my mother, with all good intentions, made every mistake in the book concerning homesickness. The day I arrived, I received four letters from Mom; she was afraid I might become homesick, but actually her letters *made* me that way. I got a letter (and more homesick) every day after that.

In one of her first letters, Mom talked about how she'd just given me a hug—she'd started the letters before I had even left for camp—and I remembered the hug perfectly. The memory did not comfort me at all. Each day, I lay hidden on my top bunk—the only place I was safe—reading her letters.

My mom is still full of little caring surprises, but I guess she learned her lesson about the letters. I just finished my first year at college, 1,500 miles from home. She wrote only once in a while, but she shows me she loves me in many other ways.

Katie, 20, Plantation, Florida

*M*y family and I emigrated from Scotland to America when I was six. There were better job opportunities for Dad here, and Mom made it seem like such a natural move to make. She quickly helped establish us in our new country and is still proud of the life she and Dad made.

When I was twelve, we took our first trip back to Scotland. For me, it was a great vacation—both foreign and familiar. I remembered all my cousins, the foods, the smell of the air, and my granma. But as we all piled into the car for the ride back to the airport, Mom started to cry, so did Aunt Nell, so did I. Then my granma began to cry end-of-the-world tears, and even my stiff-upper-lip dad looked like he was on the verge.

I later realized that our new world was possible only because Mom had left her cherished old one—her family, home, country, and mother. I think my mom is amazing.

Campbell, 46, Larchmont, New York

One cold Sunday morning, I was sent out to get raspberries for our cereal. It was so cold outside, I had to put on a coat—strange weather for berry picking. My mother had taught us well on what and when to pick. I went out to Mom's beautiful garden and I stood mesmerized by the neat and tidy rows of fruit and vegetables, some so tall, they needed sticks to help them stand up. Others were so low, we would have to look to the ground or even dig to find them. We would find vegetables in one row, fruit in another. It was always so much fun.

Suddenly, my mother yelled, "Our cornflakes are getting soggy! Dona Mae, bring our fruit!" Without realizing it, I had been staring at Mom's garden for thirty minutes, just in awe.

Mom has been one hard act to follow. I have yet to grow a vegetable garden and I am forty-eight. I miss her so.

Dona Mae, 48, Toronto, Ontario, Canada

$\mathcal{M}$y mother was witty. Stubborn. Intelligent.

Her dark eyes flashing; she distrusted a sentimental approach.

She was a brilliant researcher, playing tennis and Mozart on her violin.

My mother loved to skate, flushed with the cold air. At age seventy-six, she fell in love ... with 8th Street!

One of my last memories was her calling me, "Brigid,

I saw the Netherlandish show and one angel reminded

Me of someone. I finally remembered who ... Lolita!"

She comes back to me often, always shaking her head

And laughing. "Don't sing that again. Don't sing that thing

Again." And her pride, I feel her fierce pride.

Brigid, 52, New York, New York

$\mathcal{M}$y mother is incredibly brave and strong. She married young, wooed by my father's charms. Before she knew it, she had six children and a philandering husband. Still, I always thought she was so pretty. Mom took university courses at night, trying to better herself and to develop other interests. When four of us were grown and out of the house, and the two youngest were in their teens, Mom left my father. She was forty-five, and there weren't a lot of opportunities, but she made the best of it.

The amazing thing is how she has always been there for us, never putting herself first, but was still able to take care of herself as well. I've always been able to talk with her about everything, and our relationship just gets better as we go along.

Mary, 47, Halifax, Nova Scotia, Canada

$\mathcal{W}$hen I was fourteen I was accepted into a prestigious ballet school in New York City. Mom attended this same school and then had a fabulous career, before marrying and having children. Her scrapbook, with all the playbills from shows she danced in, showed a beautiful and happy person. I wanted to be just like her.

I worked hard at the ballet school. At the end of the year I met with my teachers. Mom came with me—I was so nervous. I was told that I would not be accepted back into the school because of my turn-out.

Afterward, I ran down the stairs, crying. When Mom caught up with me, she hugged me and said I was the best daughter in the world. She then picked my chin up and gently wiped my tears away.

I knew then that she accepted me for who I was. I later discovered jazz dance—and Mom was right there in the front row of every performance, as proud as ever.

Carolyn, 39, Irvington, New York

$\mathcal{M}$om was an only child from a poor family and a bad marriage. But she was intelligent, artistic—and eager to get away from home. Eventually, Mom won scholarships to several out-of-state colleges, but her father would not pay boarding expenses. So she commuted to tuition-free Cooper Union, and it was there that she met two significant people: her husband and Ruth.

Ruth came from a similar situation as Mom's, and the two would meet every morning before class. One look and Mom could tell what kind of night Ruth had had at home—and vice versa. They helped each other through it all.

Mom married my dad at nineteen, and though it was perhaps motivated by a desire to escape, it's been a wonderful marriage. Ruth also went on to a successful marriage and life. And in the fifty years since college, Mom and Ruth's friendship has grown and brought together their own mothers, as well as their daughters and even their daughters' daughters.

Anna, 44, Santa Fe, New Mexico

There was a lice epidemic in my school when I was in third grade and my long, down-to-my-waist hair was my pride and joy. Sure it was full of knots and split ends—but I believed I was Cinderella . . . until the school nurse discovered lice in my hair!

When Mom came to pick me up, the nurse showed her the lice eggs, called nits, and said it would be easier to go through my hair by cutting it first. I burst into tears, but Mom calmed me down, assuring me that she would never do that.

We went home, did that awful rinse, and Mom then spent hours nit-picking my hair. We talked, laughed—and sometimes I cried, because of the knots in my hair. It took weeks to get rid of the lice. Mom tried every trick—Vaseline in my hair, tea-tree oil, and slicking it back in a bun. But she never mentioned cutting it (I came up with that idea in fourth grade).

Isabelle, 18, Bellingham, Washington

*W*hen I was in high school, I went to Japan as an exchange student. Though this trip was through an established organization, my mother was a nervous wreck. I'd be so far from home, in a foreign culture, and she couldn't even imagine the host family I'd be staying with.

I understood Mom's fears and told her I'd write a letter as soon as I got there (this was way before E-mail and casual international calls). But once I got there, days passed until I found a moment to write.

Meanwhile, my host family's father, a doctor, wrote to my parents immediately to tell them I had arrived safely. But by the time the letter reached my mother, she could only think the worst. And her fears seemed to be confirmed by the father's opening line: "I am a surgeon and your son—"

Mom shrieked and threw the letter down. But Dad picked up the letter—and delivered the good news.

Mark, 55, Grand Forks, North Dakota

$\mathcal{M}$y mother was not the kind to tape spelling tests to the refrigerator or seal blue ribbons in baby books. "Love it and leave it," she would say, and toss my small accomplishment into the trash can, where it was immediately forgotten. We were six children all together—perhaps we weren't unique enough to be memorialized. When Sam, the fifth, asked for a baby picture to include in his high school yearbook, my mother could only come up with a snapshot of Andy, the first. "Just use this one," she said. "You all looked the same."

My mother was so blithely indifferent to the artifacts of memory that I was shocked to find one day, while rooting in her jewelry box for a pair of earrings, a blue plastic treasure chest filled with our baby teeth. Tiny and brittle as the bones in a starfish, the teeth were evidence that my mother cherished us, indulged in nostalgia sometimes, perhaps wished we had never grown up. Secretly, my mother loved and kept.

Kelly, 26, New York, New York

$\mathcal{W}$e moved from New York City to the suburbs when I was seven years old. It was a much easier commute for my father. For me, it was great having a yard and neighbors, but for my mother, leaving the city was really hard.

That's why every Saturday, Mom would load up a big shopping bag with dry cleaning, perhaps a shoe that needed to be fixed or an item that needed to be returned, grab her list, and head back to our old neighborhood. There, she would go to all her former shops—the cleaner's, the cobbler's, etc.—just as if she still lived there.

Dad once said, "You know, they have dry cleaners up here." Mom said, "I know, but I like my old one." She said she knew it might look silly, but it was her way of dealing with the move.

After about a year, Mom started getting to know the local merchants—and suddenly had time on Saturday for things besides errands.

Steven, 14, Matawah, New Jersey

$\mathcal{M}$y mother has always been something of a diva, and she married a French stage-and-film actor.

Once, when we were living in a fifth-floor apartment in Paris, a bomb (from some Spanish leftists) hit the ground floor of our building early one night. I looked out my bedroom window and saw flames rising. I ran to Mom and she calmly appraised the situation. Then she headed to the bathroom, announcing, "I've got everything under control," and locked the door.

Minutes passed. I tried going out our door, but beyond was just black smoke. "Mom!" I called.

"Everything's under control!" she called from the bathroom.

But I didn't think so. I forced the bathroom door open—and there was Mom, applying her makeup!

"Well, dear, there will be firemen arriving, and perhaps photographers!" she explained.

When they arrived, Mom was ready for her close-up, carefully coiffed and in her high-heeled slippers.

Antonia, 41, Paris, France

$\mathcal{R}$emember that time, Mom, when we were telling funny stories at the dinner table, eating a Hawaiian pizza with pineapple and ham, and you laughed so hard, you choked on your bite of pizza until a chunk of pineapple came out your nose?

And remember that time when I came home from junior high on Valentine's Day without a single Valentine and you had made cupcakes for us (single mom and single son) with pink frosting?

What about that time at Sea World when we were looking down into the sea lion pool and I accidentally bumped you and knocked your prescription sunglasses off your head and into the water? You told me that it was all right because you'd heard that sea lions had bad vision and might get some use out of them.

This sounds crazy, and you probably don't believe me, but one of these days I'm going to write a book and put in it all of the funny, outrageous, loving, wonderful memories of you.

Rob, 33, New York, New York

$\mathcal{O}$ne of the coolest times in my life was the summer I was twelve and in the town musical, *The Music Man,* with my mother. I played the young girl, Amaryllis, and Mom was Marian the librarian's mother. We practiced together at home, went to rehearsals together, and often went to the local diner afterward with other cast members. Since most of the cast was adult, I got to know them as friends, not just as parents, which made me feel very grown-up.

Mom and I were both having such a great time being in the play, we knew it would be a letdown once it was over. So, to give us something to look forward to, Mom reserved a room at the Drake Hotel in Chicago, where we went the weekend after the show (a big success) was over. We went shopping, took a boat ride on the Chicago River, and shared the most enormous banana split I have ever seen. An amazing time with an awesome mom.

Chiara, 20, Boulder, Colorado

*O*ne thing I love to do is to throw birthday parties for my children. I think of a theme, plan the details, then create the decorations until it's as beautiful and original as I can make it. This love I know I got from my mom, who did the same for me.

We lived in rural Connecticut and my birthday fell in February. Mom would be busy for weeks, making decorations and planning the games, party favors, and how the cake would look— different every year, but with a birthday near Valentine's Day, and my last name being Hart, the cake was always heart shaped.

Once, Mom organized a hayride, though perhaps the blizzard was extra. Another time, Mom drove us all to the Children's Museum in Hartford—a huge undertaking, I now realize, though back then it worked like magic.

And it's that "mother's magic" that I try to put into my children's parties, so that they remember the love behind the festivities, which is how I remember mine.

Suzanne, 42, Litchfield, Connecticut

Amazing and Wonderful Things about My Mom (Part 1)

She loves me no matter what. She taught me to love myself no matter what. She encourages me to stand up for what I believe in and to trust my intuition. She never left her family, no matter how hard it was. And it was hard. She was committed to her children's personal excellence. She has indulged me with life's finer things. She has taught me to give to others and to myself. She can patiently listen for a zillion hours and also tell amazing stories. She always made my friends feel at home. She is a gifted artist. She reads great books and then tells me the stories. She loves opera and still does aerobics at seventy-four. She has lived in Canada, Guam, Mexico, Italy, and Guatemala. She made sure I saw *The Nutcracker Suite,* even when money was tight. She let me pick hot-pink carpet for my room.

Jeannie, 41, Bend, Oregon